NOTHING, BUT THE BLOOD

THE GOSPEL ACCORDING TO DEXTER

Published in Los Angeles, California, by Gray Matter Books. Gray Matter Books is a trademark of Sideshow Media Group, Inc.

Unless otherwise noted, Bible quotations are taken from *The Voice Bible*, © 2012 Thomas Nelson, Inc., Nashville, Tennessee.

Bible quotations marked "NIV" are from the *Holy Bible: New International Version*, © 2011 Biblica, Inc., and Zondervan, Inc., Grand Rapids, MI.

Bible quotations marked "KNT" are from *The Kingdom New Testament: A Contemporary Translation* by N.T. Wright, © 2011 HarperOne, New York, NY.

ISBN: 978-0-9847790-2-4

CONTENTS

ACKNOWLEDGMENTS

To Kalen, my wife. In the midst of the most challenging
year of our lives, our love, commitment, and loyalty have put
down the deepest roots. I adore you more than words can
possibly express. Thank you for believing in me, endlessly.

To my girls, Gemma and Pippa. You are indescribably
wonderful to me, utterly perfect, the very joy of my life.

To Mom. You gave birth to me and gave birth to
my love for *Dexter.* You've encouraged me in my
calling from the very start. I love you so much.

To Dad. Advisor, guide, helper, *hero.* Where would I be without you?

To Redmond. Technology is most epic when used to
bless friends. And you, my friend, did just that.

To Chris. I've not met you yet in person, but your heart and your work
are an inspiration. Thank you for your writing, for Ecclesia, and for
words of encouragement that moved this project from dream to reality.

To Grant. Thank you for your brilliant design work on this
project, and for friendship and encouragement along the journey.

To proofreading and editing wizards, Dan and Beth.
Thank you for your generosity and ingenuity.

To Dwell. This is only the beginning of a deep impact made, a lasting mark, a legacy. What a ride it has been and what beauty lies in store for us in our next season. All for God's mission.

To Barb, my big sister. I miss you so much, and look forward with great anticipation to our resurrection. Your undying love and support was tangible throughout this project, even in your bodily absence.

To Nick. This is all because of you, all of it. I love you dearly, my covenant brother. You are the definition of strength and loyalty, against all others and against all odds. Together through the dark and light.

To Jesus. The Author, the Finisher.

FOREWORD

In some ways, I might be an easy, yet logical, choice for someone to preface Zach Hoag's work in *Nothing but the Blood: The Gospel According to Dexter*. I've made it a way of life to watch great films, television series, and movies, allowing those narratives to lead to deeper truths - to lead to eternal conversations.

It first started for me in the steam room of my local gym when I heard people discussing a show called *The Sopranos* every Monday. I'd never seen the show; from everything I knew from my Baptist upbringing, it wasn't a show I was supposed to watch. And yet, the first time I dialed in, I watched an episode that was entirely about heaven and hell - who's going to heaven, who's going to hell, and why. From that moment forward, I was hooked. I realized that the culture around me was having a spiritual conversation and I desperately needed to be a part of it. So I watched *The Sopranos*, week after week. Originally, my viewing had nothing to do with a book called *The Gospel According to Tony Soprano* – I simply wanted to be a part of the conversation in the steam room at my local gym.

The Gospel According to Dexter has come about in much the same way: birthed out of a desire to engage people in meaningful conversation about issues that really matter. Like *The Sopranos*, *Dexter* is, at times, a deeply troublesome show. Oftentimes, I find myself somewhat embarrassed, hoping that no one realizes what I'm watching or that no one will look over my shoulder to see what I'm watching. At other times, the show kicks into high gear and it seems to speak truth, not only to my soul but to many others as well.

13

Dexter is about justice. It reveals a longing for an imperfect kind of justice, much like Moses – after his first exposure to the oppression of his people, his impulse for justice led him into a murderous rage and he began to beat the oppressor before ultimately murdering the man and burying him in the sand. It took time, but Moses' impulses were eventually reined in when he encountered a Living God. He learned that murder was not the path for justice and came to understand that God had a more transformative and holistic plan.

I don't know that we will see the same transformation occur with the character of Dexter, but I believe that those who follow this narrative are capable of undergoing a similar journey akin to Moses, one in which we may find our longing for *shalom* ultimately fulfilled through God's divine justice. In his poignant work, *Exclusion and Embrace*, Miraslav Volf explains so clearly why we desire justice in a world filled with struggle and evil. In fact, he notes, we would struggle to believe in a God who is not wholly just:

"My thesis is that the practice of nonviolence requires a belief in divine vengeance... My thesis will be unpopular with man in the West... But imagine speaking to people (as I have) whose cities and villages have been first plundered, then burned, and leveled to the ground, whose daughters and sisters have been raped, whose fathers and brothers have had their throats slit... Your point to them - we should not retaliate? Why not? I say - the only means of prohibiting violence by us is to insist that violence is only legitimate when it comes from God... Violence thrives today, secretly nourished by the belief that God refuses to take the sword... It takes the quiet of a suburb for the birth of the thesis that human nonviolence is a result of a God who refuses to judge. In a scorched land - soaked in the blood of the innocent, the idea will invariably die, like other pleasant captivities of the liberal mind... if God were NOT angry at injustice and deception and did NOT make a final end of violence, that God would not be worthy of our worship."[1]

We share this similar longing for God to make things right. In the world today, 20 million people are currently living as slaves. Half of them are children, and many are growing up in the sex trade industry. As we learn about these kinds of evils and injustices, it elicits a reaction in us that feels a lot like *Dexter*. As I am surrounded with these stories of wrongdoing and as I went to South Asia with dear friends who were fighting for justice for children who have been sold into the sex trade, there was a significant part of me that wanted to see their oppressors die. If you don't fantasize from time to time about seeing Seal Team Six go into action against people who oppress and abuse children systematically, there is most likely something wrong with you. And yet, I'm convinced that those operating continually with the obsessive conviction that justice will come through further violence and death are even further off the mark.

As people of faith, we have to become a body that ultimately trusts in the divine justice of God. This is what *The Gospel According to Dexter* is all about.

CHRIS SEAY
Ecclesia Houston

Dexter Morgan is a Broken Man

A Man Called Dexter

"It's still there, Dex. The stain's so deep it can't be erased."

- HARRY MORGAN

"I have all the characteristics of a human being:
blood, flesh, skin, hair; but not a single, clear, identifiable emotion..."

- PATRICK BATEMAN, AMERICAN PSYCHO

Dexter Morgan is
a broken man.

As I write this, the sixth season
of the Showtime series *Dexter* has
recently come to a close. This season
featured a special emphasis on the
protagonist's grappling with issues of faith
and spirituality - a theme that's been building
since Season One, but has suddenly become
more pronounced. It's a bit of serendipitous
timing - strangely providential. While this book
is entangled in the story of a man called Dexter, it
is really about faith.

It is really about the gospel.

At the center of historic Christian theology is the gospel of
Jesus the Messiah. And the gospel of Jesus is an odd thing. To
many of us in the West, the gospel is simultaneously familiar
and unfamiliar. The ghosts of confrontational street preaching
and awkward personal evangelism linger, while televangelists and
religious pundits continue to populate the media landscape with
their power-grabbing, politicized vision of a Christian culture. If the
multitude of polls and studies on the matter are any indication, it seems
that many are sure they don't like the church because of its judgmental,
irrelevant agenda.

But this begs the question: Is any of that really the gospel at all?

19

The gospel is so close, yet so far away. It is as common as a faith-fueled commentary on FOX News, yet as strange as an oppressed Middle-Eastern people group in the first century - a people group far removed from the daily life of Western culture, but who, at the core, were simply broken people in need of rescue and restoration.

Dexter's character was created in Jeff Lindsay's 2004 novel, *Darkly Dreaming Dexter.* When Showtime adapted the novel for the TV screen in 2006, over a million viewers tuned in weekly to follow the story of Dexter, Deb, Miami Metro Homicide, and the elusive Ice Truck Killer. Five seasons later and moving well beyond the confines of Lindsay's original storyline, the show continues to grow in popularity.

The question is, Why do people find this serial killer who kills killers so compelling?

In my mind, *Dexter* is fantastic entertainment. Moreover, it's simply great art. All the key elements are in place: a riveting serial plot line, fast-paced storytelling, engaging and humorous dialogue, and dynamic character development.

Additionally, the setting is brilliant. Where shows like *CSI:Miami* perpetuate the glossy-grimy, South Beach, Art Deco stereotype innovated by *Miami Vice, Dexter* dares to give viewers a more authentic glimpse at a city that remains relatively underexposed in pop culture. I know the real Miami; I was born there, lived there until I was ten, and have often visited since then. And I can tell you that even though the show is mostly filmed in and around Los Angeles, *Dexter* just *feels* like Miami.

Miami is, after all, a tropical city lined with palm trees and bounded by famous beaches. Yet it is also a multicultural urban center with a population bursting to 5.5 million in the metropolitan area. And it is incredibly diverse: Miami is ranked first in percentage of residents born outside the country (59 percent).

Shows like *Miami Vice, CSI:Miami*, and *Dexter* do hold one message in common though: Miami is a dangerous place. It is listed among the 25 Most Violent Cities in America with a robbery rate that is triple the national average.[1] Contrary to *Dexter's* main plot, it has a relatively low murder rate, which reveals some fantasy necessary for the plot line of the show. But there is danger nonetheless, as witnessed by my own family members who have accepted home robberies and stolen cars as a fact of life. Truly, as a friend of mine recently remarked, Miami would be the absolute worst place in the world to live if, in addition to everything else, it was literally teeming with ruthless killers!

Yet, even amidst *Dexter's* fantasy, the authenticity shines through. Consider the diversity of characters. There is something so very *real* about Dexter, Deb, Masuka, Doakes, Batista, and LaGuerta. The supporting characters, mostly antagonists - from Season Three"'s bombastic Jimmy Smits to Season Four's inimitable John Lithgow to Season Six's ensemble including Mos Def, Colin Hanks, and Edward James Olmos - reflect this very same realness. It's a cultural and ethnic cross-section that defies the Hollywood tendency towards ethnic homogeneity or token diversity.

Gone are the days of Tubbs and Crockett in pastel blazers.

Dexter is artful and authentic. Yet, is this the main reason audiences find it so compelling? My belief is that while *Dexter* is definitely great art, there is actually something deeper going on in this show that keeps people coming back episode after episode, season after season. There is an element in the story of Dexter himself that resonates profoundly with all of our stories. We find a central theme in his fictional life present in the nonfiction of our everyday longings, failures, dreams, and disasters.

Dexter Morgan is a broken man. We are all broken people.

Perhaps it is best to begin this book with a look at the latest installment of Dexter's story - the faith-driven Season Six. Right from the start, in Episode One, Dexter is grappling with belief in God as he considers how he will raise his son, Harrison. Detective Angel Batista, who often acts as an earnest (if misguided) mentor to Dexter, attempts to persuade him that his son should attend a Catholic preschool. However, Dexter is concerned about the scary-looking icon affixed to the building.

> **BATISTA:** *The crucifix. That's a powerful image of the sacrifice that was made for us. All kids have to learn those kinds of things.*

> **DEXTER:** *Sorry, but why?*

> **BATISTA:** *It's the Catechism. God has put a desire for himself in every person.*

DEXTER: *Look, I know this is a little basic, but how do we even know if there is a God?*

BATISTA: *There is a God because in every one of us there is a powerful sense of moral goodness... But honestly, when you really get down to it, it's all about faith.*[2]

In this simple exchange, Batista spans the major categories of theistic apologetics: the soul's innate desire for God (the "God-shaped hole"), an inner moral law (the conscience), and the *a priori* nature of faith (belief before evidence).

Saint Augustine wrote, "You have made us for yourself, O Lord, and our hearts are restless until they rest in you."[3] Yet isn't that the problem? Batista has good intentions, but he simply doesn't understand Dexter's condition. Dexter Morgan is a broken man; for all of this talk of a soul or a conscience or a need to believe, the stark reality is that, most of the time, Dexter barely even feels *human.*

The psychological diagnosis may deem Dexter "a sociopath, or a psychopath , or an antisocial personality, or even a *dissocial personality*" (emphasis added). In Dexter, there is a direct similarity to the real-life serial killer John Wayne Gacy, Jr.; both manifest a psychopathic urge to kill with no resultant emotional connection, no apparent empathy for the multiple victims kept, in Gacy's case, under the floorboards to decompose in the crawlspace. Or in Dexter's case, under the calm, glassy surface of Bay Harbor, carefully dismembered and then tossed overboard in Hefty bags.

Philosophy professor Jerry S. Piven describes it this way: "There are breadcrumbs from the opening moments [of Dexter] that lead us to the profound psychological crises of murderers, the trauma and cataclysms that massacre their souls and set them upon quests to kill. One of these clues is the cavernous void inside Dexter. He repeatedly says that he feels empty inside. Not just unemotional, but empty. There's something missing, a hollow that he feels, as though something had been surgically removed, as if he should be filled with something and is ever feeling that space inside him."[4]

Empty. Emotionless. Soulless.

Wait. Could this be a God-shaped hole?

The aforementioned evangelists and religious pundits generally begin their story at the place of moral guilt, the place where God's law thunders down in a flash of brilliant light, throwing human failure and wrongdoing into sharp relief. They begin at Mt. Sinai.

Sinai is where Moses and the liberated Israelites received the Ten Commandments as they journeyed out of slavery in Egypt, through the wilderness, in hopes of reaching the land of promise and flourishing. It is not incidental, then, that one of the big-ticket issues promoted by the so-called "religious right" in recent years is the placement of the Ten Commandments in public spaces, often courtrooms and statehouses. All of this is indicative of a traditional morality perspective: that the bent of humanity, in general (and secular culture, in particular) is to drift further away from traditional moral values and further into moral and societal chaos. Those defending traditional morality, thus, become an "us" opposing an enemy "them." They scarcely will admit to their own failure as they point out the endless failures in society.

In their revealing work, *UnChristian*, David Kinnaman and Gabe Lyons pinpoint the perception of Christianity, the church, and the gospel that results from this: "Nearly nine out of ten young outsiders (87 percent) said that the term *judgmental* accurately describes present-day Christianity...They say Christians are more focused on condemning people than helping them become more like Jesus. Could this be telling us we have lost something in the way we articulate and describe God's expectations? Are we more concerned with the *un*righteousness of others than our own *self*-righteousness?"[5]

Within a traditional morality framework, there is but one way to view someone like Dexter: he is a killer, an immoral lawbreaker who must be stopped (and, if convicted in Texas, promptly executed). However, much to the dismay of those who hold this view, the Judeo-Christian narrative does not begin in the desert at the foot of the mountain. It begins, instead, in the lush, verdant plains of Eden. It begins at the very Genesis of our evolved human history with two real and representative human beings. Two truly and fully *human* beings: a man called Adam and a woman called Eve.

Adam and Eve were "truly and fully human" in the sense that they were whole and complete in every aspect of being alive in a human way. In spirit, mind, and body, and in all of their relationships, these first representatives were complete: perfectly at peace with all God's creation, alive with purpose. Everything was "very good"

(Genesis 1): just and right. The ancient Israelites called this state *shalom*; and *shalom* is what it means to be truly human.

A clarifying word is necessary here. This idea does *not* imply that some individuals possess more intrinsic value than others as human beings. Rather, it means that the goal of human life is to live into our true human *potential* for good, a potential fully realized by the first representative human beings, but not since then. None of us has fully arrived and that is precisely the point. That said, there are glimpses of *shalom* in all of our lives. Think of it this way: whereas one typically says, "I'm only human," when they fail at doing the just, good, and loving thing, instead one should say, "I'm truly human," when they succeed!

Theologian Scot McKnight uses the word "Eikon" to describe this concept; it's the Greek translation of the Hebrew "image" used in Genesis 1:26-27. In the biblical creation narrative, Adam and Eve, the representative human beings, were created in God's image; they were to be his Eikons, his reflective lookalikes, in the world. They were made to be bearers of what theologians call the *imago Dei*.

McKnight writes, "To be an Eikon means, first of all, to be in union with God as Eikons; second, it means to be in communion with other Eikons; and third, it means to participate with God in his creating, his ruling, his speaking, his naming, his ordering, his variety and beauty, his location, his partnering, and his resting, and to oblige God in his obligating of us. Thus, an Eikon is God-oriented, self-oriented, other-oriented, and cosmos-oriented. To be an Eikon is to be a missional being - one designed to love God, self, and others and to represent God by participating in God's rule in this world."[6]

This means that human beings were made with the potential to be whole and complete, totally at peace, in every dimension of life (spirit, mind, and body) and in every relational direction (with God, self, others, and the world).

Most of us know what comes next in the story. There was a particular tree in the center of the Garden. The Creator-God clearly told the representative human beings not to eat from the fruit of that tree because doing so would bring certain destruction and death. The tree offered power. It promised control. The man and woman believed that its fruit would make them gods-in-themselves. So, they ate; they disobeyed; they sinned; they fell.

And the ultimate consequence of all this was death entering the good world. Death - the deterioration of humanity in spirit, mind, and body, ending up in the grave. As the story goes, we all fell and died with our first representatives.

At first glance, it may appear that this story simply reinforces the centrality of moral guilt. Many draw a traditional morality perspective from this account, pinpointing the moral disobedience of Adam and Eve as the source of all the world's problems. But is there something more going on here? What exactly is the nature and significance of the beginning of this thing called *sin*, even *original* sin?

McKnight agrees with the theological perspective that views sin as something more than mere moral guilt. Particularly, it is "the universal failure to achieve our human destiny." He concludes that "sin in the Bible is the choice to 'go it alone,' to be 'free' in the sense of independence, to achieve (like God) absolute freedom.

But herein lies the problem: Eikons are made for union with God, communion with others, love of self, and care for the world. To strive for absolute freedom is to ask the Eikon to do what it cannot do. Eikons can't eikon alone. Eikons are made for relationship and to give Eikons a life without relationships, without dependence, and without love will diminish them."[7]

Relationship, not mere moral guilt, is the context for everything else the gospel is telling us. That's because all of life is fundamentally relational. The story begins in a garden with two representative, truly human beings. It continues with Adam and Eve's decision, their choice, to fracture their relationship with God, to go against the good, caring instruction of their Father. Immediately, this choice affects their view of themselves, as they feel shame and try to hide from God (Genesis 3:7-11). This leads to fracture in their relationship with each other, as they shift accusation and blame (Genesis 3:12-13). It swiftly devolves into cold-blooded murder within a generation (Genesis 4:1-8) and war, oppression, and every other social blight soon after.

Thus, the fateful choice made by the representative, truly human beings was really a choice to plunge themselves into something similar to Dexter's own diagnosis. Fallen human beings are not all serial killers (thank God), but at the root we have all chosen *dissocial* independence as our life's direction. Thus, human history itself is characterized by this dissocial downward spiral of destructive independence, with life ever fragmenting in all directions - in our relationships with God, self, others, and the world.

Sin is the rending of the very fabric that makes us truly human, a coming apart that manifests itself in ills both individual and systemic, with perpetrators and victims who multiply in the endless unraveling, generation after generation. Dexter narrates:

> The sins of the father go on and on,
> from kid to kid to kid, unless someone
> - you - chooses to end them.

As representatives, the truly human beings fell. And we all fell with them. The world is, thus, full of cracked Eikons - valuable, beautiful human beings made in God's image, but reflecting only partially the divine destiny, the true potential for which we were made. We are bent and broken bearers of the *imago Dei*.

Dexter Morgan is a broken man. We are all broken people.

What can make us whole again?

> Tonight's the night.
> And it's going to happen again and again.
> Has to happen.

Season One, Episode One begins with this ominous narration. It sets the stage for the first kill that we witness at the hands of a man called Dexter. It begins the story of a fictional Eikon, a broken image-bearer of God, caught in an endless cycle of fragmentation. In this way, he serves to exemplify the dissocial direction in which sin is taking the whole human race. In some cases, like Dexter's,

29

this path of human brokenness seems to branch off onto backroads and tributaries which, if followed, may destroy a person to the extent that there is scarcely anything truly human left.

But wait.

Right at the start of the story, we are introduced to someone else: Mike Donovan.

He's the one.

Mike Donovan is a successful boys' choir director who has utilized his squeaky-clean image as a front for something unthinkably horrific: the sexual abuse and murder of young boys. Dexter drags Mike to the kill site with a kind of anger that (we see later) is not always present in his murders. Before the kill itself, Dexter is enraged as he speaks with Donovan:

"Look. Open your eyes and look at what you did!" On one side of the room are the deteriorating bodies of Donovan's victims.

"I couldn't help myself," Donovan whimpers.

Dexter retorts, "Trust me, I definitely understand. See, I can't help myself, either. But children, I could never do that, not like you - never, ever kids...I have standards." There is disgust in his tone; indignation, even. This is a kill that Dexter seems particularly engaged in, deriving a sadistic enjoyment.

When the scene changes, Donovan is lying on a table, wrapped in plastic, shaking, trying to scream through a mouth full of gauze.

Dexter slowly brings a surgical saw down onto his throat.

> **My name is Dexter. Dexter Morgan. I don't know what made me the way I am, but whatever it was left a hollow space inside.**

Dexter Morgan is a broken man. Hollow and deeply stained.

Yet, this book aims to explore a possibility beyond this fact: that in the midst of Dexter's brokenness, something is being redeemed. Even though he "can't help it," perhaps there is actually a choice that Dexter is making in the midst of his inability and despite his damaged state - a choice that is taking him from where he is toward something better, perhaps even beginning to restore the very thing that makes him truly human.

It is hard to believe that the choice to kill could possibly count as a step in the journey out of oppression and into restoration.

It is hard to believe that the defiant posture that Dexter adopts towards God and faith - "That never helped anyone" (Season One), and, "I'm quite content to go about my life believing in nothing" (Season Six) - could actually serve as evidence for a God-shaped need in the hollow space of the shred of a soul housed in Dexter's murderous frame.

Yet there it is, in his own words. "I could never do that. Not like you." The *imago Dei* glimmers, as it were, off of Dexter's own knife.

In his follow-up book to *UnChristian*, *The Next Christians*, Gabe Lyons writes, "To many onlookers, Christianity has become a parody of itself."[8] He hones in, specifically, on the Christian tendency to engage in a morality-based culture war:

"These devoted followers regularly consume newsletters, radio shows, and magazines by Christian patriots, pastors, and pundits. If you happen across a culture warrior, you might be solicited to fight against the secularization of our nation and subjected to passionate pleas about moral decline. They are agitated to stand up for their moral convictions and vote only for pro-life and anti-gay-marriage politicians. If you disagree with their cultural posture, beware. You might be labeled unpatriotic or worse...ungodly."[9]

Additionally, most popular versions of the "gospel" - notoriously shouted on street corners, presented in forced personal encounters, or digested in awkward tracts - tend to come strictly in the form of news about the afterlife: "Many are bound to a Gospel story with a climax that feels actually quite boring. 'Go tell others how to escape from Planet Earth' doesn't feel like a compelling mission..."[10]

If the story begins in the Garden with truly human beings living a whole and complete life of peace in a world that is good, then these modern "gospels" are confused. If all of life is relational and the core problem is relational brokenness, then culture warring will only do more harm than good. All of this says that there is a gospel "fog" blanketing the land. Perhaps *Dexter* can provide an illustration for what the gospel really *is*, however unlikely that may seem. Perhaps this TV show (that has become a cultural phenomenon) can provide us with a breeze strong enough to help clear away the fog.

There are many facets of this man called Dexter yet to be explored in these pages, and each chapter will focus on one. Each part of Dexter's story will, in turn, shed light on a part of the gospel itself. *Dexter* is rich with these gospel reflections and they even go beyond the character himself, becoming especially brilliant in light of his relationships, his community, and his politic (yes, his politic). But I am getting ahead of myself.

For now, take a moment to reflect on the broken man who can't help killing. Like real-life killers, to a devastating degree, he is disconnected from his own humanity. But he is only a few steps further down the path that all of us have traveled, away from the wholeness, the *shalom*, that a loving God desires for us, that existed in the beginning.

As Sufjan Stevens sang of real-life killer John Wayne Gacy, Jr.:

And in my best behavior
I am really just like him.
Look under the floorboards
For the secrets I have hid.[11]

We are all broken people.

That's where the gospel begins.

Something
New
Is
Needed

2

A Son Called Dexter

"We have been called to heal wounds, to unite what has fallen apart, and to bring home those who have lost their way."

- ST. FRANCIS OF ASSISI

I serve as lead pastor of a young, missional church called Dwell[1], located in the "least religious state" in the US: Vermont.[2] On top of that stellar title (which ought to replace "The Green Mountain State" on our license plates), *Men's Health* magazine recently rated our city - Burlington - the least religious *city* in the US![3] This makes sense, really. Burlington is Vermont's largest city, a college town, full of vibrant culture and art and not so full of church-goers.

My story is not unlike many others. I was raised in a Christian home, and my dad was a pastor when I was growing up. It is sometimes strange to look at my adult life so far and see how much it mirrors my dad's. Though I once swore to myself that I'd never be a church-planting pastor, I'm following in his footsteps, almost to a T! The especially great thing is that my dad is a central part of my life and ministry now, so his presence and influence continue to shape and guide me.

Yet, there is a way in which my journey is different from his, especially because of the time and place in which I am learning to minister. My dad began his ministry during the transitional time of the 1980's in Miami, FL, with a church community facing particular cultural challenges. I find myself ministering here in Burlington - least religious city, least religious state, second decade of the 21st century.

37

And the cultural transition underway during my father's church-planting experience has come to something of a fullness now. The life and work of our church has emerged in a new context, a truly post-Christian or "post-Christendom" one, requiring a new perspective and new approaches. I am taking all that my dad has given me, and I am endeavoring to make it my own.

One thing remains the same though. I have a father who is always there. I have a father who loves me.

Dexter Morgan is a broken man.

A broken man with a father.

A father who loves him.

There is no *Dexter* without Harry Morgan. Early in the series, Harry's words transform Dexter's story from one of darkness and despair to one of hope, however faint. "Remember this forever," Harry says to young Dexter in an Episode One flashback. "You are my son. You are not alone. And you are loved."

Those are powerful, life-shaping words.

Those are *gospel* words.

They are spoken in response to a teenage Dexter's progressive realization and disclosure of his insatiable urge to kill. So far, he's fulfilled his desire only with animals, but he feels the urge towards people too.

Harry is shockingly patient towards his adoptive son, unreasonably understanding. He is not approving, but he is *gracious*.

The "scandal" of the Christian gospel is precisely that God is patient, longsuffering, and unconditionally loving, despite his grief over human wrongdoing. As an adoptive Father, he is unreasonably understanding. Perhaps nowhere in the biblical narrative is this more evident than in Jesus' own story of the "Prodigal Son."

Presbyterian pastor Tim Keller is quick to remind us of the real meaning of "prodigal" - and its potential double usage - in his essential book *The Prodigal God*. He writes, "The word 'prodigal' does not mean 'wayward' but, according to Merriam-Webster's Collegiate Dictionary, 'recklessly spendthrift.' It means to spend until you have nothing left. This term is therefore as appropriate for describing the father in the story as his younger son.'"[4]

The story itself is found in Luke's Gospel, chapter 15. The father in the story is a well-to-do estate owner with two sons. The father represents God; the sons represent all of us. The older son is seemingly loyal and devoted to the family business while the younger is so careless that he breaks traditional family ties by demanding his vast inheritance immediately. Many will recognize the phrase from the old King James Version: "the younger son... wasted his substance with riotous living" (verse 13).

Essentially, he emptied his entire trust fund partying. Hard.

After all was spent by this *prodigal* son, he returned home to apologize and seek a job as a mere servant on the estate.

"So he got up and returned to his father. The father looked off in the distance and saw the young man returning. He felt compassion for his son and ran out to him, enfolded him in an embrace, and kissed him. The son said, 'Father, I have done a terrible wrong in God's sight and in your sight, too. I have forfeited any right to be treated as your son.' But the father turned to his servants and said, 'Quick! Bring the best robe we have and put it on him. Put a ring on his finger and shoes on his feet. Go get the fattest calf and butcher it. Let's have a feast and celebrate because my son was dead and is alive again. He was lost and has been found.' So they had this huge party" (verses 20-24).[5]

With this story, Jesus intended to show his first-century audience that God was Father in a way they had not yet grasped. He was not simply the authoritarian, the patriarch, to be honored and obeyed. Instead, he was the *prodigal* Father, ready to cast off custom and dignity and run to hug and kiss his broken, screwed-up children before they could even blurt out their apology. Ready, indeed, to spare no expense on a lavish party for those very same kids.

Dexter Morgan is a broken man. A broken man with a father who loves him.

Roughly a thousand years before Jesus told his parables, Moses ascended the mountain.

A lover of his people, the Israelites, Moses had recently found himself exiled from the land of Egypt where he had been adopted into great power and wealth as a child. The situation had unraveled. In an act of vigilante justice, he struck an Egyptian slave-driver for striking an Israelite slave. The Egyptian died, and Moses fled in fear for his life to the deserts of the Sudan, where he married and settled into a blue-collar life of shepherding. Soon he would end up in another place, leading the entire Israelite slave population out of Egypt and into the wilderness, by way of a Red Sea crossing so spectacular that neither Cecil B. DeMille nor CGI could ever do it justice. How did this happen? How did Moses successfully subvert the Egyptian empire without ever again picking up a weapon?

Answer: *God.*

The great claim of the Exodus narrative in the Hebrew scriptures is that there is a King mightier than Pharaoh. There is One who supersedes any and all human empires. *I AM* is his name because that's all you need to know. He is perfect, pre-existent, existence itself. He is the pristine definition of goodness and justice. He is who he is. Period.

God identifies himself at this early juncture in the biblical storyline as the Rescuer-God. And the implication is simple: people are in need of rescue. The Israelites in Egypt were victims of economic injustice, slavery, genocide, and sexual exploitation. They were victims of systemic brokenness and sin. They needed rescue, and God is the Rescuer-God.

Yet, we remember the connection further back in the narrative. The situation in Egypt is a macrocosm of the situation in Eden. The same drive to be "like gods" is present there. This radical, destructive independence developed into a quest for absolute power, no longer symbolized by a forbidden tree, but a pyramid skyline, an empire of selfish power and control. The dissocial agenda of the

41

Egyptian empire was part of the same process of deterioration that began when the representative human beings made that initial fatal choice, fracturing their humanity in all relational directions - with God, self, others, and the world.

However, we can't limit the effects of human brokenness to macro-level genocide, whether in ancient Egypt or modern-day Darfur. It obviously includes that, but it goes deeper than that. There are surely some evils that are far greater than others, and we never ought to downplay the difference between victim and victimizer when such evil rears its ugly head. Yet, all are guilty of evil at some level, however small. Keller reminds us: "When a newspaper posed the question, 'What's Wrong with the World?' the Catholic thinker G.K. Chesterton reputedly wrote a brief letter in response: 'Dear Sirs: I am. Sincerely Yours, G.K. Chesterton.' That is the attitude of someone who has grasped the message of Jesus."[6]

And what exactly is Jesus' message? "[J]esus says: 'The humble are in and the proud are out' (see Luke 18:14). The people who confess that they aren't particularly good or open-minded are moving toward God, because the prerequisite for receiving the grace of God is to know you need it."[7]

The Apostle Paul adds, "You see, all have sinned, and all their futile attempts to reach God in his glory fail" (Romans 3:23).

Or in the words of musician David Bazan:

It's hard to be
A decent
Human being.[8]

Simply, we are all broken people. We all fail to reflect the glory of God, which is our true human potential. This is where the gospel begins, after all. We are bent and broken bearers of the *imago Dei*, and we've all contributed, in greater or lesser ways, to the direction of humanity as a whole down the road of becoming less than truly human. The road leading to more and more destruction. The road leading to disintegration and deterioration. The road leading, in the end, to death.

We all need rescue.

And it is in light of this relational brokenness that Moses ascended the mountain.

In order for the rescued Israelites to become a community of rescuers themselves and not just perpetuate the same cycle of brokenness that they observed in the Egyptian empire, God needed to impart something of his perfect existence, of his goodness and justice, into the identity of the people themselves. Moses ascended Mount Sinai because the Rescuer-God had something to give to the people. Guidelines for a new way to live.

The Ten Commandments.

The Ten Words.

The Decalogue.

These Ten, along with numerous supporting laws and rituals, together formed a robust rule of life for a newborn community of hope in the fallen world.

You might call it: *the Code.*

In Season One, Episode One we are introduced to a set of standards given to Dexter by his adoptive father Harry. Throughout the series, these standards are referred to as "the Code of Harry," "Harry's Code," or, simply, "the Code." Dexter is vitally connected to the Code as the ethical anchor keeping him safe, sane, and good. It is the reminder that a healthy society does exist, a society of which Dexter is not naturally a part, but within which he may live and move - so long as the standards are followed.

There is a sense, too, that the Code gives Dexter a unique opportunity to begin to live in a more human way. One of the key rules, and the foundational premise of the entire show, is to "never kill an innocent." Dexter must kill only those who are killers themselves and show signs that they will kill again. Note Harry's words to teenage Dexter after he admits to killing animals:

"You're a good kid, Dex - you are. Otherwise it would have been a lot worse than animals. We can't stop this, but maybe we can do something to channel it. Use it for good."

There seems to be an essential goodness, but a stronger essential brokenness. In Harry's view, if that brokenness can't be healed, at least it can be bent back towards the good, enacting justice in the world and restoring some sense of Dexter's humanity. In other words, if Dexter can't obey the sixth commandment, "You are not to murder" (Exodus 20:13), at least he can enforce it: "Whoever sheds the blood of a human, that person's blood will be shed in return by another, for God made humanity in His own image" (Genesis 9:6).

And that's precisely the point: the purpose of Harry's Code is not to change Dexter's predisposition towards murder. The purpose is to restrain or redirect it. The purpose is to apply the straight edge of justice to the jagged lines of Dexter's psyche; to encourage conformity as much as possible for the greater good of Dexter and others. For Dexter, though, the Code is "a set of standards that keep me from getting into trouble" (Season Six, Episode One). Dexter is devoted to Harry's commandments, to be sure, but there is a persistent tone of dispassionate rule-keeping, of detached obligation.

Fans of the series know that this dispassion and detachment present a brilliant opportunity for comedy. As all the people in Dexter's life fret over moral dilemmas and live in a whirlwind of ethical drama, Dexter seems to glide through it all with his half-cocked grin and stiff disposition perfectly intact. He flies above the clouds with coffee and Cuban sandwich in hand. Yet, he must try to fit in; after all, the first rule of the Code is, quite simply, "Don't get caught." So he desperately analyzes social cues and the emotional subtleties of his family, friends, and co-workers in order to blend in better.

> People fake a lot of human interactions, but I feel like I fake them all, and I fake them very well. That's my burden, I guess.

On not a few occasions, he misses the joke or smiles at the misfortune, to the bewilderment or disgust of those around him (which is great fun for us as viewers). At one particularly gruesome murder scene in Season Two, Deb asks Dexter, "This stuff never gets to you?" To which he tactfully replies, "I'm more of a crying-on-the-inside kind of guy." Dexter is chronically unaffected, which is often hilarious.

In all of this, one thing becomes clear. As vitally connected as Dexter is to this Code, it is yet part of the social mask. It is merely one more layer in an external disguise. The Code is a babysitter for a man otherwise out of control.

In the New Testament letter to the Galatians, the apostle Paul looks back and comments on the law of Moses from the perspective of the first century CE, and especially in light of the recent advent of Israel's purported Messiah, Jesus. Paul refers to the life, death, and resurrection of Jesus as his "faithfulness to the covenant." This means that he lived a life of total fidelity to his divine destiny, fully reflecting the Father's glory and demonstrating wholeness in every relational direction - with God, self, others, and the world. He lived a truly human life as the "second Adam."

The idea is that because he was faithful, there is hope for all of us who have been unfaithful. We are all broken people, often acting out in ways that chip away at our potential for true and full humanity. We are victims and victimizers, all of us. But there is someone who has lived the truly human life as our new representative.

In chapter 3 of Galatians, Paul writes, "Before this faithfulness arrived, we were kept under guard by the law, in close confinement until the coming faithfulness should be revealed. Thus the law was like a babysitter for us, looking after us until the coming of the Messiah, so that we might be given covenant membership on the basis of faithfulness. But now that faithfulness has come, we are no longer under the rule of the babysitter. For you are all children of God, through faith, in the Messiah, Jesus" (verses 23-26, KNT).

The law given to Moses at Sinai, contained within the five books of Moses, is summed up in the word "Torah." Through Torah, the rescued people of Israel were given an opportunity to stand out in the midst of a world of oppressors. They could begin to bend the broken image back to the goodness of God's original intent for his creation and, in so doing, give witness to God's justice in an unjust world. They could be a blessing to others. The law was to be deeply ingrained in the identity of this community, an ethical anchor to keep them safe, sane, and good.

Yet, as the story unfolds, it becomes clear that ancient Israel simply would not live up to the task. While there was an essential goodness, the stronger brokenness worked itself out in the same acts of abuse and injustice common to the rest of the world. Religious hypocrisy was rampant. Later in the story, the Israelite prophet mourns:

"I hate - I totally reject - your religious ceremonies and have nothing to do with your solemn gatherings…Here's what I want: Let justice thunder down like a waterfall; let righteousness flow like a mighty river that never runs dry" (Amos 5:21, 24).

And that's because Torah was really only the beginning of the story. It was only the first phase of the full rescue. It was not complete in itself. It was not sufficient for the task of bringing God's peace and justice to the world.

Scholar N.T. Wright says, "Torah had a purpose all right; it was indeed God's holy law; but its purpose was to keep Israel in check, to stop

God's wayward people from going totally off track, until the time when, through the Messiah, the long-term promises could be fulfilled."[9]

Both Paul and Wright are saying that there was something deficient about the law. It was not meant to last. It was a temporary, external restraint meant to curb wrongdoing but not necessarily heal the essential brokenness.

Sound familiar?

The Code of Moses, like the Code of Harry, purposed and important though it was, was yet only good enough to guide God's community to the better thing that was coming.

The complete rescue. The way to become truly human again - all through the life, death, and resurrection of Jesus.

The result is summed up in this simple yet sublime thought: "For you are all children of God, through faith, in the Messiah, Jesus."

We are all broken people, people with a Father, a Father who loves us.

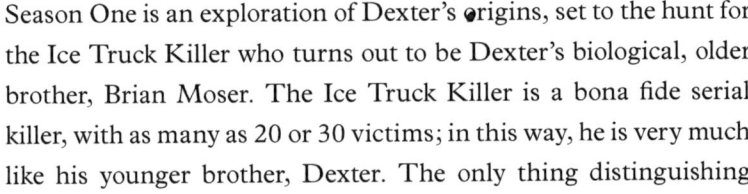

Season One is an exploration of Dexter's origins, set to the hunt for the Ice Truck Killer who turns out to be Dexter's biological, older brother, Brian Moser. The Ice Truck Killer is a bona fide serial killer, with as many as 20 or 30 victims; in this way, he is very much like his younger brother, Dexter. The only thing distinguishing them, really, is the Code.

That and Harry Morgan.

Both Harry's adoptive love and Harry's ethical Code are essential to Dexter's grasp on his thin humanity; without them, he would be all but lost, much like Brian. Yet, as the *Dexter* storyline continues to unfold in Seasons One through Three, it becomes clear that, despite his sincere promise and intent, Harry Morgan did not live up to the ideal of unconditional love. He was not a truly prodigal father. His love and his Code were indeed the start of Dexter's rescue, but their weakness was eventually exposed.

Dexter's father, in other words, was not like *my* father, a man of faithfulness and courage. He did not follow through on his promise and make good on his covenant. I am blessed because mine did.

Dexter says it best in a Season One narration:

> I built my life on Harry's code. I lived by it. But Harry lied. Why would he do that? What else don't I know? My concrete foundation is turning to shifting sand.

Harry lied about the circumstances surrounding the trauma that created Dexter and Brian's murderous urges. He lied about his affair with their mother, Laura Moser. He lied about the fact that Laura was a paid informant for Miami Metro Homicide, supervised by Harry and placed into a perilous situation with a drug cartel, which directly resulted in Laura's brutal murder right in front of her two boys. He lied about the fact that he was the first detective on the scene to find Brian and Dexter inside of a shipping container, sitting in a massive pool of blood from their mother and three other

49

chainsaw victims - where they had been for several days. Most of all, he lied about Dexter's older brother Brian, whom he committed to an institution as a "f***ed up kid," keeping him from Dexter, who had forgotten about him due to post-traumatic stress.

Was Harry's adoption of Dexter simply out of obligation to Laura and guilt over the fact that he was partly to blame for her death? Was the Code anything other than superficial? Did Harry believe that Dexter could actually live a more human life? The father tips his hand in a Season Two flashback, after young Dexter comes out of a session with a child psychologist:

> **HARRY:** *You really impressed me in there today, son. I don't know how you did it, but great job.*
>
> **DEXTER:** *I just pretended to be someone else.*
>
> **HARRY:** *Well, it's working. Keep doing it. I mean, that doctor didn't even see the monster inside of you!*

Young Dexter's countenance falls as he realizes what his father sees in him: a monster. An incurable darkness.

It would appear that Harry and his Code present a good, though imperfect, parallel to the first-century Israelite's understanding of God and his law - and, really, for the common 21st-century person's concept of what God may be like. Is God mainly concerned with condemning and, hopefully, curbing immoral behavior? Is he the religious pundit railing about keeping the Code on courtroom walls? More to the point, does God really love broken people? Does he really forgive broken people? Can he really *believe* in broken people?

Too often, the Christian faith is reduced to an exercise in external, exclusive, prideful religion. It was this precise problem that the rabbi Jesus sought to untangle and deconstruct through his interactions with the religious establishment of his own day. His solution to the problem is exemplified so clearly in that story of a shockingly prodigal God. And the world needs Jesus' solution desperately.

Really, Harry's Code is kind of like an "old covenant." Something new is needed.

"'So,' you ask, 'does the law contradict God's promise?' Absolutely not! Never was there written a law that could lead to resurrection and life; if there had been, then surely we could have experienced saving righteousness through keeping the law. But we haven't" (Galatians 3:21-22).

"Remember, if the first covenant had been able to reconcile everyone to God, there would be no reason for a second covenant... With the words 'a new covenant,' God made the first covenant old, and what is old and no longer effective will soon fade away completely" (Hebrews 8:7, 13).

A new kind of covenant-relationship is needed, one with a Father who truly loves us, truly accepts us, and would spend anything and everything to rescue us, to make us truly human. A Father who sends his own precious Son as the representative for all his lost children, a Son who empties and spends himself to redeem us, being "obedient to death - a merciless death on a cross." A Son born to die, *born in blood*, so that all of us could be *born again*.

Moses ascended one mountain: Sinai, the place of the law. Jesus ascended another: Calvary, the place of the cross. The rescue that began at that first mountain comes to maturity at the second. A new exodus out of slavery and into true freedom is accomplished there. Only at the second mountain do we see the fundamental relational problem that began in the lush, primordial Garden solved; without it, there is only the law's external restraint, leading to despair, failure, guilt, and darkness.

Could a person like Dexter Morgan - or even Brian Moser - ever experience the full rescue, the full redemption of their true humanity? If the pundits spend their breath railing against a lawless society, with implicit and explicit words of condemnation for the sinful "them," how does Jesus' new covenant message provide an answer?

"...Jesus' message, which is 'the gospel,' is a completely different spirituality. The gospel of Jesus is not religion or irreligion, morality or immorality, moralism or relativism, conservatism or liberalism. Nor is it something halfway along a spectrum between two poles - it is something else altogether. The gospel is distinct from the other two approaches: In its view, everyone is wrong, everyone is loved, and everyone is called to recognize this and change."[10]

We are all broken people. The gospel starts there and then gives us hope. "In the king, and through his blood, we have deliverance - that is, our sins have been forgiven - through the wealth of his grace which he lavished on us" (Ephesians 1:7-8, KNT).

We are already loved. Lavished with grace.

Already forgiven. Totally. Completely.

Through the cross, relational peace is made in every direction because the full weight of our destructive independence was already placed on Jesus the Messiah, our representative in life and death.

It is finished.

We are free.

And because of that, *change is possible.* The prodigal Father believes in us. The monster can be defeated. We can begin to become the human beings we were made to be.

"If you, Lord, kept a record of sins, Lord, who could stand? But with you there is forgiveness, so that we can, with reverence, serve you" (Psalm 130:3-4, NIV).

Pastor Chris Seay reflects on the lost, prodigal son in a sermon:

"I wonder the last time that you were consciously aware that you felt lost, you felt alone. I wonder how you'd live...[if you were to be] welcomed and be completely forgiven. How do you live in response to that kind of love? What does it call us to?"[11]

In Season Six, Episode Eight, Dexter follows an investigative lead to a senior-living community where he tries to solicit information from an old priest named Father Galway. The priest has advanced dementia and seems to be of little use, except that he asks Dexter to confess his sins.

Dexter hesitates. He confesses to breaking the speed limit "a few times."

The old priest urges him on: "Anything you confess, God will forgive."

DEXTER: *I've killed people.*

FATHER GALWAY: *Continue.*

DEXTER: *A lot of people.*

FATHER GALWAY: *Murder is a mortal sin. You must…you must…where were we?*

DEXTER: *Confession.*

FATHER GALWAY: *Yes, of course. I absolve you of all your sins, in the name of the Father, the Son, and the Holy Ghost. Amen.*

DEXTER: *Thank you.*

Perhaps this old, senile priest gives us a glimpse at the prodigal God. He absolves us of all our sins, no matter how severe, how mortal. It is almost as if he forgets them. He gives that kind of grace to the humble, to the ones who know they need it - like Dexter does. "Your wrongdoings are bloodred, but they can turn as white as snow. Your sins are red like crimson, but they can be made clean again like new wool" (Isaiah 1:18).

How do we live in response to that kind of love?

What does it call us to?

This kind of gospel is the one that informs our community of faith in Burlington - a gospel of unconditional love and forgiveness that calls us further into our true humanity. Our task is to reflect the prodigal Father as we do life in the least religious city, in the least religious state, in 21st-century post-Christendom America. We aren't perfect, but we are learning to embody this kind of good news better.

As I once remarked to a local journalist, "The foundation of our community is love and friendship. We don't want to be judgmental, self-righteous bastards."[12]

Despite Harry's shortcomings, he has lovingly imparted the Code.

Dexter has learned much from him.

Yet the time has come for Dexter to take what his father gave him and make it his own.

From
the
Garden
to the
City

3

A Father Called Dexter

"We've all got both light and dark inside us. What matters is the part we choose to act on. That's who we really are."

- Sirius Black, Harry Potter and the Order of the Phoenix

I am getting to "that age."

The age that, as a kid, you think you will never, ever reach. It's the age that brings gray hairs (plural - they have not yet overtaken the other hairs so as to be considered the dominant hair-party), a slower lifestyle, unforeseen additional pounds, and achy joints (for me, especially in the feet). The age that brings marriage and a career direction and "settling down."

And, sometimes, children.

There is no more concrete milestone that I have found for the transition into "capital A" Adulthood than the act of becoming a parent. Truly, one does not need to become a parent in order to be an adult, and there are many parents who are merely adults in the biological sense. But broadly speaking, among relatively healthy and stable people, something happens to a person when he or she becomes a parent. It is a little like being shot out of a cannon into a new realm of responsibility, selflessness, and maturity.

And above all, love.

I remember how it happened for me. For the nine or so months leading up to my first daughter Gemma Grace's arrival on January 7th, 2010, my wife and I were participants in a strange game of make-believe: *What do you think it will be like when she arrives? Will she have dark hair, do you think? Who will she look like most – you or me? I'm a little nervous – will life change that much? What about our relationship, will we still be as close and do the kinds of things we love to do together? Will there still be romance?*

Really, it was all a dream. There was nothing tangible except a swelling, moving belly - which was strange, to be sure, but not exactly life altering.

Then she arrived.

It is difficult to describe such a thing in anything-less-than-epic language. She was indeed "born in blood," and, by the end of the ordeal, the delivery room looked a little like Dexter's kill room, with a surprising amount of spatter. I had watched my wife go through something of a death - expulsive pressure and explosive pain - in order to bring about a completely new life. Something like a resurrection.

With Gemma's new life came a new life for my wife and I, as well. We were still "us," but we also were something completely new. We would not lose the identity that we shaped as a young couple, but this identity would be expanded into something more. In fact, from the very start, we found ourselves becoming more than we ever thought we could be, with a capacity for love, compassion, care, and justice that we had not yet dreamed possible. All because of little Gemma.

Simply because there were now three, we were suddenly, unexpectedly, becoming more alive in a truly human way.

I can pinpoint the exact moment it happened. We took Gemma out of her swaddle, put on her first outfit, and strapped her into her car seat. The nurse checked the straps to make sure they were tight. We loaded Gemma into our car and drove away from the hospital. Right then, it hit me.

I'm a father.

During my first watch of Season One, I was delighted by the odd relationship between Dexter and Rita Bennett. Rita remains one of my favorite characters in the series, despite her lack of dramatic flash and flare. In fact, it is precisely her simplicity that makes her so important to the storyline. Rita is the guiding light of the first four seasons, another anchor that reminds us we are still tethered to goodness, truth, and beauty and not hopelessly adrift on the bloody waves of Bay Harbor.

To say that Rita exhibits an ethical simplicity does not mean that she lacks any depth of character. She is not the suspicious morality police, nor is she the naive, dumb blonde. Instead, it is her emotional nuance that makes her so compelling. She is at once broken and trusting, wounded and innocent, soft and strong, forgiving and righteous. When she makes her first appearance in the pilot, it is, in a way, like a sudden breath of fresh air after a long night in the stifling swamp of death.

Actually, it is *exactly* like that.

The door swings open. She is not gorgeous, but she is lovely. Her brown eyes reassure us. Her bright smile eases the tension of the

61

brutal story to which we have just been exposed. Her voice is shockingly sweet: we need that voice; we come to love that voice.

The relationship between Dexter and Rita is immediately endearing for its innocence. Rita had been in a sexually abusive marriage with crack-addict Paul before meeting Dexter (in fact, that's how they were introduced); and, at the start of her relationship with Dexter, she is nervous about this new journey, hesitant to let go of the past and give way to this future. Combine all of that with Dexter's inherent awkwardness and the result is fumbling, giggly conversation and bumbling, sweet attempts at intimacy. And when Rita's fear of being intimate is made clear, her new boyfriend is patient and supportive. Rita is amazed by his kindness.

The viewer mustn't forget, though: Dexter Morgan is a broken man.

We've been dating for 6 months now. It's perfect because Rita is, in her own way, as damaged as me.

Because of his brokenness, Dexter isn't much interested in sex anyway; he just doesn't get it. Rita's damage is convenient. And Rita, of course, is none the wiser: "I can't believe I found the one good, truly decent man left on the planet."

See, the apparent innocence is endearing until we realize that this relationship is all part of Dexter's mask, formed and fashioned by the Code of Harry: *don't get caught, try to blend in.* In a Season Five flashback to Dexter's first date with Rita, it is humorously obvious.

The restaurant Dexter chooses has nothing to do with the food, the atmosphere, or the company. As Rita nervously rambles on about Caesar salad, Dexter's gaze drifts to his real date: Marcetti, a killer he is stalking.

But is that it? Is that all there is to this picture? Even in the early episodes, there is a hint of something more. Something beyond the surface show, a crack in the facade, introducing reasonable doubt. It's there when he's with Rita, and it's especially there with the kids.

The kids are Astor and Cody, Rita's children from her marriage with Paul. When Dexter is with them, the viewer seems to forget the monster entirely. When he is with them, his behavior is not forced, it is not strained, it is not awkward. It is natural, joyous, easy.

Simply put, something happens to Dexter as he assumes the role of father.

The final episode of Season Two closes with Dexter's narration:

As it turns out, nobody mourns the wicked...
I think Harry knew that from the start. That's
why he gave me a Code. It cost him his life,
but it kept me alive through incredible trials.
The Code is mine now, and mine alone. So too
are the relationships I cultivate. They're not
just disguises anymore. I need them. Even
if they make me vulnerable. My father might
not approve, but I'm no longer his disciple.

63

> I'm a master now. An idea transcended into life. And so this is my new path. Which is a lot like the old one, only mine.

Dexter is taking what his father gave him and making it his own.

Much transpires in Season Two that leads Dexter to this conclusion, not least of which is his unfaithful fling with 12-step program sponsor Lila West. Lila is the temptress, an edgy Brit with Keira Knightley looks and a dark secret of her own. She drives an obvious wedge between Dexter and Rita, almost bringing their relationship to a destructive end. All of this is set against the backdrop of Miami Metro Homicide's manhunt for the "Bay Harbor Butcher" - Dexter himself.

In the end, Dexter and Rita are reunited; the crack detectives blame the tens of murders on Agent Doakes and not Dexter; and Lila, now revealed to be a murderous arsonist obsessed with Dex, meets a fitting end in her London flat at the edge of Dexter's blade. "I've got a plane to catch... You've killed an innocent man," he says, laying her down on the couch, plunging the knife into her heart, and zipping up the plastic bag.

We've already compared the Code of Harry to the Law of Moses, showing both to be incomplete and prone to weakness. Here, at the close of the second season, Dexter expresses a very similar thought. Something new is needed, a new Code owned and embodied by Dexter, himself. Moreover, a hallmark of this renewal - this new path, this idea transcended into life - is Dexter's avowed *need* for relationship.

This is our first hint at the healing of his deep, dissocial brokenness.

The people in his life are not just disguises anymore.

The prophet Jeremiah announced a coming renewal:

"Look, the days are coming when I will bring about a new covenant with the people of Israel and Judah. It will not be like the covenant I made with their ancestors long ago when I took them by the hand and led them out of slavery in Egypt. They did not remain faithful to that covenant - even though I loved and cared for them as a husband. This is the kind of new covenant I will make with the people of Israel when those days are over. I will put My law within them. I will write it on their hearts. I will be their God, and they will be My people. No longer will people have to teach each other or encourage their family members and say, 'You must know the Eternal.' For all of them will know Me intimately themselves - from the least to the greatest of society. I will be merciful when they fail and forgive their wrongs. I will never call to mind or mention their sins again" (31:31-34).

According to Jeremiah, the hallmark of this new covenant – which, while different from the old one, remains continuous with it - would be its location and expression. Namely, it would be *located* in people's hearts and not on external tablets of stone, like the Ten Commandments. And it would be *expressed* in a relational body of people intimately connected to God and one another. Mercy and forgiveness would define the renewed covenant-relationship.

The new Code, as it were, is an idea transcended into life through a people, no longer just a babysitter or mere restraint.

No longer a facade of rules.

Beyond rule-keeping, the new covenant is one of holistic *restoration*. Jeremiah joins the other prophets of the Hebrew scriptures in an overwhelming emphasis on this. Their words are pregnant with the pain of human brokenness and the longing for true healing in the world. They all seem to point to a time when this will happen - when God will finally "satisfy those who are weary and...refresh every soul in the grips of sorrow" (Jeremiah 31:25) and all people on the earth "will hammer their swords into sickles, reshape their spears into pruning hooks" and "not practice war anymore" (Isaiah 2:4).

While at first glance it might appear that the prophets were just speaking about some temporary peace for ancient Israel, it becomes clear that their vision is, in fact, much bigger:

"The Eternal, Commander of heavenly armies, is preparing a feast, a feast for everyone on this mystical mountain with aged wine and good food, the finest wine and choicest meat. And God will swallow up the oppression that weighs us down. He will take away the heavy shroud that is draped over all peoples of the world. God will swallow up death forever. The Lord, the Eternal, will wipe away the tears from each and every face and deflect the scorn and shame His people endure from the whole world, for the Eternal determined that it should be so. And in that moment, at that glorious time, people will say, This is our God! We put our hope in him. We knew that He would save us! This is our God, the Eternal for whom we waited. Let us rejoice and celebrate in His liberation" (Isaiah 25:6-9).

This restoration will be a celebratory feast for everyone, all peoples of the world. It will include such things as the death of death itself. There will be no more sorrow, no more tears of pain, no more injustice and oppression. There will be a full and final liberation of the world from its own brokenness, at the hands of I AM, the Eternal, the Rescuer-God.

This brings us back again to that primordial Garden, to those representative truly human beings. Because that's what we want the world to be and more. As one theologian puts it, the beginning of the story was home, the middle was home-wrecking and homelessness, and the end will be homecoming. The Garden home is the climax as well as the opening scene. In fact, the very last book of the Bible gives us the "Garden 2.0," the perfectly renewed world, now symbolized by a City:

"I looked again and could hardly believe my eyes. Everything above me was new. Everything below me was new. Everything around me was new... And I saw a holy city, the new Jerusalem, descending out of heaven from God, prepared like a bride on her wedding day, adorned for her husband and for His eyes only... The prophecies are fulfilled: He will wipe away every tear from their eyes. Death will be no more; mourning no more, crying no more, pain no more, for the first things have gone away" (Revelation 21:1-4).

I wonder if this vision of the world's restoration has not been almost completely lost on generations of church-going people in the West. I wonder if the loss of this vision is the primary contributor to the confusion over the true nature of the gospel, because that gospel continues to elude us. We desperately need to climb our way out of the muck and mire of a rule-based, power-grabbing version of the

67

good news (which is not really good news at all). Equally, we need to come down from a "pie-in-the-sky" evangelism that saves souls from a future, nebulous hell while ignoring the hells of our present, broken world (which is not good news, either). Perhaps the way forward is this holistic, life-affirming gospel of restoration.

If Harry Morgan was the beginning of Dexter's salvation, Rita Bennett starts the process of a deeper restoration.

Her intimate, trusting relationship with him (even though she is never fully aware of his identity) is precisely what he needs to begin the process of healing. His coming into relationship with a family, assuming the role of a father, is a sudden, cannon shot forward on the path to wholeness. Because of Rita, Dexter is able to leave the confines of the external Code. He is able to internalize the Code's justice, shed its immaturity, and put it in its proper context. He begins to reinterpret Harry's law at a heart-level, to see all in light of the relationship, in light of the love he is beginning to understand.

Harry tried to restrain Dexter, but Rita helps Dexter to confront the monster within.

His *Dark Passenger.*

The Dark Passenger is Dexter's way of describing the dark urge to kill that lurks inside of him. It is possibly the most pervasive and powerful theme in the show. The Dark Passenger is vital to our understanding of Dexter's psyche - that he is consciously aware of a conflict going on within him, a battle raging between light and darkness. For the most part, his task until meeting Rita, Astor, and Cody has been to channel the darkness so that he doesn't get caught. Yet, the darkness has been overwhelmingly powerful. The Dark Passenger has, in fact, been the one in control of Dexter's life more often than not.

Which brings to mind the apostle Paul's confession in Romans, chapter 7:

"In my mind, I am in happy agreement with God's law; but the rest of my body does not concur. My bodily members are at war with my mind (which agrees with the law), and I have become a prisoner in this war to the rule of sin that reigns supreme in my body. I am absolutely miserable! Is there anyone who can cut me free from this corpse that is tied to my back? It is slowly killing me. I am so thankful to God for the blessings of our Lord Jesus, the Liberating King! On the one hand, I devotedly serve God's law in my mind; but on the other hand, in my flesh, I serve the principle of sin" (verses 22-24).

Rita is the beginning of Dexter's realization that, perhaps, the light within him has a fighting chance.

Dexter's introduction at a 12-step meeting in Season Two is telling:

"I just know there's something dark in me. I hide it. Certainly don't talk about it. But it's there. Always. This Dark Passenger. How when he's driving, I feel alive. Half-sick with the thrill, complete wrongness. I don't fight him. I don't want to. He's all I've got. Nothing else could love me, not even, especially not me. Or is that just a lie the Dark Passenger tells me? Because, lately, there are these moments that I feel connected to something else. Someone.

It's like the mask is slipping, and things, people, that never mattered before, are suddenly starting to matter. It scares the hell out of me."

Much later in the series, Brother Sam will say to his friend Dex, "I know about your darkness, but I also see your light."

The story begins in a Garden and ends in a City.

In between are two mountains (really, more than two, as we will see) - Sinai and Calvary. Those mountains are part of the larger storyline. The problem is not mere rule-breaking and moral guilt; the problem is that we are *relationally* broken people living in a broken world, fractured in our reflection of God's glorious wholeness.

Both reason and experience confirm that we all carry a Dark Passenger of sorts, a sinful "corpse tied to our back," and the trick is figuring out how to cut our true selves free from this burden. How can the light win the battle against the darkness within us? While answers to the problem abound, and many of them are at least partially valid, the Christian gospel proposes one overarching answer: Jesus, in his life, death, and resurrection.

We have touched on the way this works, but some more explanation is in order so that we can find our way through the gospel fog that lays heavy all around us. We have seen that because of our unfaithfulness to the covenant relationship with the Creator-God - resulting in disintegration in our relationships with self, others, and the world (a dissocial spiral of destructive independence), - Jesus entered as our second representative, the second Adam. He lived a life of wholeness, reflecting the glorious goodness of the Father (a truly human life). He did this *for the world*, in place of all of us. He did what we will not and cannot do as broken people.

If we have failed the law, not just by transgressing it, but by misinterpreting and misusing it, Jesus shows us what it means to embody its heart and essence. Throwing off the immaturity of external restraint, the incarnate Son makes the law of Moses his own, an "idea transcended into life." He expounds this new way to live on yet another mountain in a famous Sermon (more on that later). He summarizes it in two Great Commandments.

Love God.

Love your neighbor.

That's really all there is to it.

In all of this, he does exactly what Jeremiah was looking forward to. He embodies a better Code written on the heart - God's love and justice in the flesh, *par excellence*. He represents us in living the truly human life. But the end game is not merely representation - it is restoration. The life he lives must somehow be transferred to us. And the only way to accomplish this is for Jesus to identify with us fully. There must be complete solidarity with broken humanity, not only in life, but also in death.

"The very likeness of humanity, He humbled Himself, obedient to death - a merciless death on the cross!" (Philippians 2:7-8).

On the cross, Jesus accomplishes this full identification. We are all broken people, and our chosen brokenness earns us death, as we choose after the pattern of our first representatives in the Garden. We kill and we die. We oppress and we die. We rage and we die. We war and we die. We lust and we die. We covet and we die. We hate and gossip and gorge and divide and lie and coerce and hoard and waste and exploit and abuse. And all through life, we experience a degree of deterioration in spirit, mind, and body which all ends up in death. The great surprise of our destructive independence, large or small, is that, while seeking to master the world and make it a slave to our own pleasure (to be like gods, to possess power), we are mastered by it instead - and it kills us.

"Beware: the day you eat the fruit of this tree, you will certainly die" (Genesis 2:17).

The Christian gospel makes the claim that the prodigal Father loved us by sending his Son - his second Self - to carry the full weight of the world's destructive independence upon himself.

The law couldn't do the trick, but God could: "For God has done what the law (being weak because of human flesh) was incapable of doing. God sent his own son in the likeness of sinful flesh and as a sin-offering; and, right there in the flesh, he condemned sin" (Romans 8:3, KNT).

In the person of Jesus, God lovingly died in place of his wayward children, paying our price, annulling our debt, setting us free.

That happened at the second mountain.

Yet, as scandalously beautiful as that is, it is not the end of the story.

The evangelists may go from mountain to mountain, but the story goes from Garden to City. What happened *after* Calvary may actually be the most important thing. Incredibly, this Jesus, this person fully-alive-in-a-truly-human-way, God's second Self in the flesh who was executed in apparent defeat - *lives again*.

He rose victoriously from death three days after his execution.

He was vindicated as fully just and good.

He was completely restored in his true humanity, never to die again.

"Death will be no more" (Revelation 21:4).

Dexter Morgan is a broken man.

By becoming a father, he begins to be restored.

It starts with Rita, Astor, and Cody. It continues with a child of his own: Harrison.

The significance is not lost on the viewer.

Harrison.

Harry's son.

Simultaneously, we watch Harry himself leave the cinematographic realm of lens-filtered flashbacks to come rushing into Dexter's present. No, he is not back from the dead. Rather, he comes to life as part of Dexter's own renewed conscience, the Code now living within him - written, as it were, on his heart. Dexter now finds himself able to discern what is just and good by reasoning and debating with the inner Code of Harry.

When the inner Code cautions him against marrying Rita and raising a family because it will make him vulnerable to being caught, Dexter pushes back and chooses his own path.

Relationship, and love, has brought the commandment to life in a whole new way.

Instead of the external letter, Dexter now embodies the spirit of the Code.

"The law of the Spirit of life breathes into you and liberates you from the law of sin and death" (Romans 8:2).

Perhaps no scene better captures this than Dexter's proposal to a pregnant Rita in Season Three. Dexter enters the living room of her house and says, "My life has always felt like an unanswered question. A string of days and nights waiting for something to happen, but I didn't know what. Rita, we're connected. Wherever I am, I feel you and the kids with me. You're what makes me real."

Jesus rose from the dead.

When he did, all those who trust him rose from death too.

This is what is meant by the Christian rite of baptism. It is not, as some imagine, simply the act of washing away old sins and becoming morally pure. That is, actually, something more like an old covenant washing ritual. But the new covenant rite of baptism is different. Baptism is about *joining* Jesus in death, burial, and resurrection (see Romans chapter 6).

It is about the transfer of his resurrected, restored, truly human life to us.

First, we go down into the water by faith, showing our solidarity with Jesus in death and burial. When he died, our sin, failure, brokenness, and fragmentation died with him. Then, we come up out of the water by faith, showing our solidarity with Jesus in resurrection. When he was vindicated as just and good when the Father raised him from the dead, we were vindicated too. When he experienced the full restoration of his true humanity - in spirit, mind, and body - so did we.

At first glance, this might seem strange. In what possible way can we receive the transfer of something like resurrection life when we trust the Messiah and express that trust through baptism? Some "gospels" answer by pointing to the future: the transfer is dormant until after you die. It only takes place after death with the receiving of a pardon and eternal life in heaven. Yet if this is really about resurrection and restoration, then it must be about *this world*, just like those ancient prophecies and images were all pointing to.

Moreover, if Jesus already rose from the dead, then it must mean something was *already set in motion*, and we can connect to that in the present by faith.

The truth is, "the presently embodied life before death can at last be seen not as an interesting but ultimately irrelevant present preoccupation, not simply as a 'vale of tears and soul-making' through which we have to pass to a blessed and disembodied final state, but as the essential, vital time, place, and matter into which God's future purposes have already broken in the resurrection of Jesus and in which those future purposes are now to be further anticipated through the mission of the church... Salvation, then, is not 'going to heaven' but 'being raised to life in God's new heaven and new earth.'"[1]

Simply, through connection with Jesus by faith, we begin to feel his resurrection life in us wherever we go.

He answers our deepest question and begins to make us real, alive.

Truly human.

"If the Spirit of the One who resurrected Jesus from the dead lives inside of you, then you can be sure that He who raised Him will cast the light of life into your mortal bodies..." (Romans 8:11).

He begins to heal our brokenness in every relational direction - with God, self, others, and the world. Love and justice are formed deep within us, written on our hearts. We enter an ongoing, transformative process enabling us to become a part of transforming the world around us. And this is what gets me most excited, right along with the old prophet: *the gospel connects us to a community of faith,* so that the love and justice of the new covenant are expressed through a relational body of people intimately connected to God and each other.

"I will be their God, and they will be My people."

They are a people on a mission to bring healing to this world, in this essential, vital time and place, little by little, neighborhood by neighborhood, anticipating the final restoration of all things.

When I became a father, something *happened.* I knew that a change was underway within me. I knew that God was doing something, restoring more of what is broken inside me.

The curtain of darkness was pushed back further, allowing that much more light to come through.

In the words of Jack Nicholson in *As Good as It Gets,* one look at my little Gemma Grace made me "want to be a better man."

As a father, I want my little girl to catch a glimpse and come to know what God is really like, and what the world is meant to be, through my life and example. That is an unbelievably high calling, urging me forward toward my true humanity. And this cuts to the core of what the gospel is. Chris Seay encourages us parents to represent the gospel well: "We have the chance to explain that shalom was broken in Eden, that Jesus restored shalom within our hearts with his sacrificial love, and that God can bring wholeness again to this broken world."[2]

That gospel is a beautiful thing.

It is hard to tell where the writers are taking Dexter's storyline. I, for one, am rooting for the possibility that it continues the trend towards healing. But I'm not convinced.

In the final episode of Season Four, we are left breathless at the death of Rita Bennett. Her brutal murder marks a tragic turn in the wrong direction. She was the beginning of Dexter's restoration, the show's guiding light, and she is gone now. What can make Dexter whole again?

Just moments before Dexter discovers her lying motionless in a bathtub filled with her own blood, with their infant son Harrison crying on the bloody bathroom floor next to her, Dexter reflects:

> I wonder if Rita is looking at this same moon, at this same moment. I like that. Connected by light. The Dark Passenger's been fighting against it, trying to keep me all to himself. But it's my turn now, to get what I want. To embrace my family. And maybe one day not so long from now...I'll be rid of the Dark Passenger.

We hope this may still be true for Dexter Morgan without Rita; but even if it is not true for him, it may yet be true for each one of us.

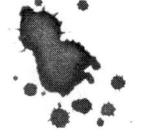

Dexter Morgan is Out for Blood

4

A Hero Called Dexter

You can run on for a long time,
You can run on for a long time,
You can run on for a long time,
Sooner or later God'll cut you down.

- JOHNNY CASH

Dexter Morgan
is out for blood.

So far, we've surveyed his essential
brokenness, examined his fidelity to
Harry's Code, and watched his movement
towards wholeness with Rita and the kids.

**She made me think for the
briefest moment that I might even
have the chance to be human.**

But what about the dark urge itself?

What about the hunt, the kill?

What about…the blood?

**Blood. Sometimes it sets my teeth on edge,
other times it helps me control the chaos.**

While blood occupies the very center of Dexter's identity, it's not in the same way that it might for a vampire or parasite. Blood is not a form of sustenance or basic stimulation for Dexter. Rather, it is a *symbol* of what actually sustains and stimulates him. For Dexter, it is the act of taking life that so viscerally thrills him; blood, powerful though it may seem, is merely the symbol of the act. Blood is the banner Dexter waves, the anthem he sings. It signals the arrival - or the afterglow - of his greatest pleasure.

Beyond addiction, blood is also Dexter's art. It draws out an aesthetic delight in him, especially when he is engaging in his day job as a blood spatter analyst for Miami Metro Homicide. From fresh crime scene to red-string spatter reconstruction to lab coat murder reenactment to microscopic blood cell analysis, Dexter is enthralled by that which repulses others. For him, it is so much more than gore and goo.

The addiction and the art converge in Dexter's most precious possession - a box of glass slides, each dotted with blood, hidden behind the cover of an old-style air conditioner in his Miami apartment. Dexter takes a blood sample from each of his victims to remind him of the thrill they gave him as he took their lives. And each slide is a thing of beauty in itself, a clean, miniature masterpiece in translucent red.

Many of us remember the Amish school shooting that occurred in Pennsylvania on October 2, 2006.

On that horrific day, Charles C. Roberts, IV entered a schoolhouse in Nickel Mines, Pennsylvania and murdered five Amish girls, aged

7-13, before taking his own life. Five other girls were wounded. Although the gunman's motives were not totally clear, it appears he was plagued by fantasies of molesting young girls and was equipped to be in the schoolhouse for a long time, presumably to abuse his victims. Instead, under pressure from police surrounding the site, he rushed to the kill.

One thing, however, is clear: he was out for blood.

Janice Ballanger, Deputy Coroner for Lancaster County, Pennsylvania, said that "there was not one desk, not one chair, in the whole schoolroom that was not splattered with either blood or glass. There were bullet holes everywhere, everywhere."[1]

When we move from a fictional killer to a real-life killer, we are sobered by the heaviness of death. That is what blood symbolizes - death. Or more accurately, it symbolizes life. Its expulsion from the body, its coming out into plain sight, oozing dark red, is *life leaving*, going out, bringing on death. "You see, the life of the body is in the blood..." (Leviticus 17:11).

As shocked as we were to hear of this brutal intrusion into the life of a peaceful separatist community, we were more shocked by what came after.

Forgiveness.

85

Along with a local nonprofit group, I am privileged to be a part of an initiative that addresses the problem of human trafficking through micro-enterprise in Moldova, a small country located adjacent to Romania and the Ukraine.

Worldwide, it is estimated that there are upwards of 30 million people in slavery today, more now than at any other time in human history. In impoverished Moldova, sex trafficking is especially prevalent. Moldova, formerly part of the Soviet Union, is the poorest country in Eastern Europe and an infamous trafficker of enslaved children and young women.

The young women, particularly, are forced into prostitution around the world or sold to private buyers for ownership and abuse. The victims of trafficking are typically orphans who are pushed out of the state-run homes at age 16. With little education and no job experience amidst a devastated Moldovan economy, they are especially susceptible to the lure and enticement of traffickers. It's quite systematic: traffickers are waiting in the wings for the next crop of youngsters to age out. Sometimes, corrupt orphanage officials will even alert the traffickers to the best targets. Before long, these vulnerable young women may find themselves in a brothel in Amsterdam or Las Vegas, or worse, in the possession of a perverted millionaire or Mafioso. The story repeats itself again and again.

Specifically, our initiative works in Moldova to provide opportunities to at-risk women through a clothing factory in the capital city of Chisinau. The factory produces hand-tailored garments that are sold wholesale or matched with limited edition graphics from a collective of artists and designers and then sold online. A large portion of the sales are then reinvested into these women and other anti-trafficking organizations. More factories and products are planned for the future.[2]

In a documentary called *Nefarious*, produced by one of our partners, there is an account of a brothel in another trafficking hotbed, Thailand. It is heart-wrenching. We learn that a seven-year-old girl had been sold by her parents to the brothel in order to generate income for the family. There is a systemic cycle of desperation and exploitation at work there. In a police raid on that brothel, the child's dress was found in one of the rooms, stained with blood from her abuse.[3]

There is no greater injustice, no more vicious form of oppression, than this.

We have already explored Dexter's standards, the Code that he comes to embody. Together with his dark urge to kill, they create a man driven by justice. Yet, what kind of justice is this?

At first glance, it is the stuff of a shoot-em-up action flick or graphic novel storyline. Harry sets it up quite well: "Son, there are people out there who do really bad things. Terrible people. And the police can't catch them all." Right in the Pilot episode, a vigilante is born, not unlike the moment when young Bruce Wayne stands over his murdered parents on a city street. The point is simply that justice must be served and public servants aren't sufficient for the task. Whether it is Gotham City or Miami Beach, there comes a time when a hero is needed.

A Dark Defender.

87

Such is the moniker that Dexter earns in Season Two as Miami Metro is hunting for the man responsible for tens of dead bodies found dismembered in Hefty bags at the bottom of Bay Harbor. When it is revealed that every single one of those bodies belongs to a killer of innocents, the citizens of Miami begin to view the mysterious serial killer who kills killers as a hero, not a villain. The comic book store owner in Episode Five explains the Dark Defender this way: "Stalker of the night, his blade of vengeance turns wrong into right."

And we resonate with the citizens of Miami on this. There is something deep within us that knows this is necessary. Vengeance. Retribution. Justice.

This is especially true for those who seem to always get away with their crimes. We want to see them brought down. We want to see their mafia empires crumble. We want to see their totalitarian regimes implode. We want to see them waste away even as they have wasted the lives of so many innocent others. We want to see them pay. Sometimes, we want to see them die.

If that seems harsh or overstated, consider those five Amish girls. Consider the exploited teenage orphans in Moldova. Consider the helpless Thai child who had her innocence, her sanity, her spirit, her humanity, her hope, progressively torn away from her rape by rape. As a father of two precious little girls, I do not hesitate in saying that I would be out for blood. Many of you would be too.

Dexter simply doesn't make any sense without this element of justified vengeance. As much as we may want the main character to find healing and restoration, we could not cheer for him without cheering for his mission of retribution. Our inner sense of justice tingles every time he thrusts the blade or swings the claw end of the hammer into the deserving body of one of his victims. We may not want to admit it, but something about it just feels *right*, however we may cringe. This Dark Defender is, indeed, fixing something about the world every time he rids it of one more killer, one more agent of destruction and death. He may not obey the commandment to not murder - but, man, does he know how to enforce it.

For this reason, I take issue with the interpretation of some who would identify the show's genius as its "sustained romanticization (even fetishization) of death." According to this view, *Dexter* helps us to mythologize death in order to make it seem less frightening and less real. *Slate* writer Katy Waldman admits, "Sure, I hate my mortality as much as the next person, but for some reason I can't summon up the requisite sense of horror at the thought of lying on this serial killer's table." That is, Dexter has made death so stylish with his compulsive, almost "erotic" brand of violence that one begins to think it would not be that bad to find oneself at the end of his knife.[4]

Dexter's violence is stylized, to be sure. This makes the show more watchable than it would be if, perhaps, the producers had taken a grittier approach. However, the genius is not that the show's style softens death's blow, nor that overexposure to violence and gore desensitizes us to its weight. The genius is that *Dexter's* violence, however stylish, resonates with our deep-seated sense of justice.

Dexter, himself, is an extreme case study in a powerful aspect of the *imago Dei* that all human beings share - the desire to set things right, to balance the scales.

Admittedly, the question of Dexter's self-conscious commitment to justice is not so cut and dry. In other words, although the deed may be just (enacting the just punishment for the crime, balancing the scales), Dexter's motive may not be. We have seen that Dexter is bound to the justice of Harry's Code, but what evidence is there that Dexter, himself, is a just person? He is out for blood, addicted to the kill. And if his killing is merely to appease the Dark Passenger, to satisfy the dark urge, then surely he is not just - not at all. He is merely using justice as a front for his own twisted ends, a disguise for his real intention. At the root of it, he is out for blood for its own sake, not as a means of making things right.

Certainly, an argument could be made to this effect. Yet, the writers have crafted a storyline that doesn't allow for this conclusion either. From the outset, the Code is presented as the beginning of Dexter's own salvation. Harry begins the training process precisely because Dexter is a "good kid" with a strong connection to his adoptive parents. He doesn't want to kill innocent people because, in his words, "I thought you and Mom wouldn't like it."

Further, Dexter's first human kill is Nurse Mary. She had been trying to kill Harry by overdosing his morphine. So Dexter acts in defense of his father, at his father's urging. If Dexter were merely a capricious psychopath, Harry would have no reason to believe that he would not kill *him* at any moment. Yet there is relationship from the beginning, even if it is not at once matched by deep and authentic human feeling.

And, as we have seen, the authentic human feeling does come. Dexter begins to be restored in his true humanity, especially by his relationships with Rita and the kids. Dexter makes the Code his own and embodies it in a heartfelt way, with relationship and love at the center of its interpretation.

His commitment to kill only those who have already killed innocent people and show signs that they will kill again is rooted in an authentic commitment to justice. Even though this choice to kill appeases the Dark Passenger's bloodlust, it is, yet, a necessary step in Dexter's journey out of slavery. As Dexter whispers to an infant Harrison, "Wanna know a secret? Daddy kills people. Only bad people. I haven't really got anybody else I can tell about that, you know? Daddy is not going anywhere, buddy. I already lost my innocence. I'm not gonna sacrifice yours too."

Yes, he kills…but he also cares.

There is light within him.

In Season One, Episode Two, there is a flashback to a conversation between teenage Dexter and his father Harry. It concerns the recent acquittal of the man who killed Harry's partner. It is, in my opinion, the definitive moment in the entire series.

> **DEXTER:** *Bad guy kills a cop and nothing happens? That's not fair.*

> **HARRY:** *Life's not fair, Dexter.*

> **DEXTER:** *Can't anyone do anything? Can't you do anything?*

HARRY: *No. Not now.*

DEXTER: *So what then – the world just keeps spinning out of control?*

HARRY: *No. The world can always be set right again.*

In this, we get a clear glimpse at Dexter's own ingrained desire for justice. And we get a glimpse at the core of the gospel itself. If nothing else, the gospel of Jesus is communicating one central message: *the world can always be set right again.*

God has a lot of stunt doubles.

What I mean is that there are many people claiming to be speaking his words and doing his deeds in the world. Many of them get at least part of it right, while some of them seem to worship a different God altogether. Indeed, some of them make one think, *If God is like that, I don't want to have anything to do with God.*

One of God's purported stunt doubles is the "Universally Vengeful God." These days, it seems the most extreme version of the Universally Vengeful God comes to us from Westboro Baptist Church, a fundamentalist group (in my view, a cult) out of Topeka, Kansas. Westboro is well-known for picketing the funerals of American soldiers killed in action and protesting outside unsuspecting synagogues in various cities across America. Their reasoning? Because "God hates America" for its pro-gay stance, and "God hates Israel" for killing Jesus.

Lovely.

On September 1, 2009, Westboro paid a visit to my home state to protest the recent gay marriage legislation. Not ones to waste a trip, they also picketed a soldier's funeral and a local synagogue in Burlington. I happened upon the synagogue protest while running errands and, knowing full well who the picketers were, felt the sudden urge to find a side street and park the car. With my heartbeat accelerating, I approached the scene.

On one side of the street were the Westboro folks, flanked by police officers who seemed concerned that things might get ugly. On the other side of the street (the synagogue side) were counter-protesters holding up cheeky signs and yelling as loud, if not louder, than the unwanted guests. The Westboro message was not surprising. All sorts of strange anti-Jewish sentiment was expressed on tacky, colorful signs, while chants and songs (I think one went to the tune of "We are the World") flowed in almost-choreographed succession. I looked at one of the female officers as if to ask for permission to speak to one of the Westboro women, and she nodded. The woman I spoke to was Jael Phelps, daughter of Shirley Phelps and granddaughter of Westboro leader Fred Phelps.

To be honest, I was so nervous at first that I forget the exact words with which I started the conversation. In essence, I asked this: "Don't you think it's kind of silly to say that God hates Jews since Jesus was, in fact, Jewish?"

Jael's response was quick: "Jesus was the Son of God and the Jews killed him."

I gathered courage:

93

"He was also the Son of Man. David's son, Joseph's son. Fully human, fully Jewish. Everything he said and did was in the context of first-century Judaism, and the movement he led was precisely the Messianic movement anticipated by Jewish people at the time…"

The more I talked, the more she talked over me, and I realized that our conversation had quickly devolved into an opportunity for her to test out her hateful Westboro one-liners.

At that point, I just looked at Jael and said, "I don't know you, but I sense that you have a good heart. I'm sorry you believe these things. There are a lot of Christians who don't believe what you all believe. And we are praying for you."

She replied, "There are a lot of 'Christians' who are going to hell."

In a world of stunt doubles, we are looking for the real God. What is he like? Is he anything like the Universally Vengeful God touted by my conversation partner? While Westboro is an extreme case, there are softer variations of this version. The common theme is God's overwhelming anger towards any and all human beings from the moment they are born. They are sinners by nature and by choice, and even the smallest sin - a lie, perhaps - is tantamount to murder or rape in God's economy. In the courtroom of the Universally Vengeful God, all are infinitely guilty and equally worthy of his wrath, the full expression of which is an eternity in the fires of hell.

The Universally Vengeful God demands this kind of absolute, unflinching "justice."

He is out for blood.

And there are other stunt doubles. At the opposite end of the spectrum, there is the "Universally Overlooking God." While there are variations here, too, the common theme is that God loves all and, therefore, all will eventually be accepted by him in an eternal embrace. The good, the bad, the just, the unjust, the advocate, the abuser - everyone will find themselves equally accepted when all is said and done. In the courtroom of the Universally Overlooking God, all destructive choices are given a pass and pardon, the full expression of which is an eternity of bliss in heaven.

Pastor and author Rob Bell suggests a version of the Universally Overlooking God. Clearly, there is much good in his suggestion, and it is *not even comparable* to Westboro in its negative effects. However, it is, yet, a stunt double that misses the mark. Bell proposes this question:

"God has a purpose, something God is doing in the world, something that has never changed, something that involves everybody, and God's intention all along has been to communicate this intention clearly. Will all people be saved, or will God not get what God wants? Does this magnificent, mighty, marvelous God fail in the end?"[5]

His answer is, implicitly, No - *Love Wins.*

Even though these two models appear to be polar opposites and have such different effects, they actually share a common emphasis. They are equally fixated on the judicial aspect of God's character and the afterlife destination of human beings. They are equally agnostic about the relational (covenantal) aspect of God's character and the realness of present choices that have lasting, permanent consequences. Both of these result in a form of the gospel that may be profoundly misshapen.

My conversation (if you can call it that) with Ms. Phelps got around to the idea of a context - a first-century Jewish context for understanding Jesus. As it happens, this context exposes the popular stunt doubles and sheds much light on who God really is. We've seen some of this already. And perhaps the most remarkable characteristic that emerges in light of this context is the *justice* of God.

It is not universally vengeful or universally overlooking.

And, thank God, it doesn't look at all like Westboro.

Which is why, after Jael's last comment about Christians going to hell, I walked away.

As I did, the female officer nearby turned to me and whispered, "Thank you."

The Dark Defender may serve as an apt illustration of God's justice.

At least one aspect of it.

The *retributive* aspect.

If the world is to be set right again, then retribution must play a part. Something deep within us knows this, because something deep within God requires this.

Dexter's "kill room" is where retribution happens, where a pure form of justice is dealt to those who truly deserve it. Since the law cannot catch everyone (and is often compromised by red tape and corruption), Dexter emerges as an almost superhuman avenger, an angel of death. His standard is absolute certainty of his victims' guilt; his punishment is swift and severe. If we were to imagine God in his role as Judge enacting the sentence commensurate with the crime, Dexter is not too far off the mark. (Dexter has even slyly hinted at such: "If God is in the details, and if I believed in God, he's in this room with me.")

There is something else about Dexter's retribution that is reflective of God's retributive justice. As mentioned, Dexter's is a relational, heartfelt brand of retribution. In the early series flashbacks we learn that Dexter's first known animal kill was a dog, Buddy, "the Billups' dog." Young Dexter didn't kill Buddy merely for the thrill, but also to stand up for his mother, Doris, who was dying of cancer: "The dog was a noisy little creep, Dad. He was barking all night and mom couldn't sleep and she's very sick..." This theme continues to the Nurse Mary flashbacks.

This form of retribution doesn't stop when Dexter is an adult. The theme of relational justice is present in the Season One story arc, when the Ice Truck Killer is revealed as Brian Moser, Dexter's own biological brother. While a part of Dexter wants to join his brother in the freedom of giving in completely to the Dark Passenger, he cannot because he must protect his innocent sister Debra. She is next on Brian's list. So Brian is next on Dexter's.

As the storyline progresses – and as Dexter begins to experience healing and restoration – the kills become more meaningful, more integrated into his humanity. Relationship, love, and passion for the world as it should be come to define his vengeance. In the Season Four finale, he finally brings Arthur Mitchell, the dreaded Trinity Killer responsible for over 100 murders, into his kill room. He reaches beyond Arthur's crimes to bring an additional accusation: that Arthur destroyed his own family, depriving them of "their future, their dignity, their hope," driving his own daughter Christine to suicide. Dexter doesn't realize that Arthur has nearly destroyed Dexter's family, too, leaving Rita to bleed out in a bathtub.

Arthur lashes out: "You think you're better than I am?"

Dexter responds, "No. But I want to be."

Deb, Rita, and the kids have given Dexter a relational context for his retributive justice. It is retribution bound up in love. "I have a family, too, Arthur. And I'm good, for them."

Perhaps the most poignant example of Dexter's increasingly relational brand of justice occurs in Season Three, Episode Three. There we are introduced to a convicted pedophile named Nathan Marten. Nathan stalks Dexter's stepdaughter Astor, first approaching her in the grocery store, then taking pictures of her at the beach. Dexter sees the monster inside of him. So strong is Dexter's bond with Astor that he commits a rare breach of Code. He has no evidence that Nathan has ever killed a victim, but as Nathan scans pictures of Astor on his computer in his home, Dexter approaches stealthily, wrapping the cord around his neck from behind.

There is a lion-like ferocity in his grip.

"I am not like you," he says.

He grits his teeth with righteous indignation.

Nathan falls from his chair and slumps to the ground, motionless.

Dexter Morgan is out for blood.

A Dark Defender.

An angel of death.

After all, "The payoff for a life of sin is death" (Romans 6:23).

The justice of God requires retribution. A payment for victimized Amish girls, Moldovan orphans, Thai children. A payment for those abused by mafia thugs or slaughtered by genocidal regimes. A payment, even, for hearts broken by hate-filled words on picket signs at the funeral of a loved one.

"When people are crushed, wronged, enslaved, raped, murdered, the Eternal is just; He makes the wrongs right" (Psalm 103:6).

In one of Jesus' parables, there is an image that bears a striking resemblance to our protagonist. It is the Parable of the Unfaithful Servant, and the master represents Jesus, the Messiah, himself. He entrusted the servant with the responsibility of managing people and affairs justly - being a good and decent co-leader in the estate.

99

The servant takes advantage of his power:

"But suppose the servant says to himself, 'My master is taking a long time in coming,' and he then begins to beat the other servants, both men and women, and to eat and drink and get drunk. The master of that servant will come on a day when he does not expect him and at an hour he is not aware of. He will cut him to pieces and assign him a place with the unbelievers" (Luke 12:45-46).

All that's missing are the Hefty bags.

If the gospel has been distorted by some as political and graceless words of judgment from a righteous "us" towards an enemy "them" - words drifting towards universal vengeance, - the solution may seem to be a sort of moral agnosticism, universally overlooking wrongs done. Scholar N.T. Wright pushes back on this latter tendency, something he calls a "depressingly flabby" theology of "easygoing tolerance":

"But judgment is necessary - unless we were to conclude, absurdly, that nothing much is wrong or, blasphemously, that God doesn't mind very much. In the justly famous phrase of [Yale theologian] Miroslav Volf, there must be 'exclusion' before there can be 'embrace': evil must be identified, named, and dealt with before there can be reconciliation... God is utterly committed to set the world right in the end. This doctrine, like that of the resurrection itself, is held firmly in place by the belief in God as creator, on the one side, and the belief in his goodness, on the other. And that setting right must necessarily involve the elimination of all that distorts God's good and lovely creation and in particular of all that defaces his image-bearing creatures."[6]

God is a father entangled in relationship with the world he has made, broken though it may be. He loves the world; he loves people. His justice is his unrelenting determination to set the world right again. His passion to protect.

To defend the defenseless. The widowed. The oppressed. The orphaned.

To punish the guilty. The abuser. The oppressor. The murderer.

The gospel includes this.

The gospel can't overlook this.

Because the gospel is all about setting the world right again.

"Now, instead, he commands all people everywhere to repent, because he has established a day on which he intends to call the world to account with full and proper justice by a man whom he has appointed. God has given all people his pledge of this by raising this man from the dead" (Acts 17:30-31, KNT).

A day is coming. You might say, a kill room is prepared - for some. He will judge with justice.

More than 30 members of the Amish community attended the funeral of the killer, Charles C. Roberts, IV. His wife, Marie, was invited to the funeral of the victims. The Amish folks extended words and gestures of comfort and reconciliation. They spent time with the killer's family members, crying with them, serving them.

The world was stunned.

In response, Marie wrote, "Your love for our family has helped to provide the healing we so desperately need. Gifts you've given have touched our hearts in a way no words can describe. Your compassion has reached beyond our family, beyond our community, and is changing our world, and for this we sincerely thank you."[7]

How did they do this? How could they move beyond vengeance to this place of forgiveness? How was it possible?

An Amish farmer described the killer this way to his children:

He had a mother
and a wife and a soul,
and now he's standing
before a just God.[8]

If we are to see God himself and not just his stunt doubles, we have to take the whole biblical narrative into account, in its original, Jewish context.

Pastor Chris Seay provocatively asks, "Is God excited about denominational loyalty, partisan politics, or pious appearance? Does God desire any of this? Is it possible that we have ignored Jesus - our wild, messianic King - and chosen to re-create Jesus in the image of the Pharisees themselves?"

He continues: "What if we, the church, were so uninformed about basic foundational teachings of the historic Christian faith that most of us could not even attempt to articulate the gospel?"[9]

The "gospel" of a Universally Vengeful God promises that a small, exclusive group of especially pious people will escape the fires of hell by the skin of their teeth while the rest of the world burns. The "gospel" of a Universally Overlooking God promises that choices in this life are not all that crucial because this earthly life is a drop in the bucket that will be followed by an eternity in which the good, the bad, and the ugly are all made good anyway. Plowing through these categories and rushing ahead as a beautiful third way beyond them is God as he really is, with a life-affirming gospel of setting the world right again.

This gospel must include a retributive kind of justice, reserved for those who have made real, destructive choices in this life that have brought real damage to God's good world and the humans that he loves. However, there is another aspect of God's justice that supersedes retribution. As illustrated in Dexter's own journey of becoming truly human, the defining characteristic of God's justice is not retribution but *restoration*.

"Do I enjoy watching the wicked die? No. I, the Eternal One, would prefer for the wicked to stop doing the wrong things they do and live" (Ezekiel 18:23).

"So here is the result: as one man's sin brought about condemnation and punishment for all people, so one man's act of faithfulness makes all of us right with God and brings us to new life. Just as through one man's defiant disobedience every one of us were made sinners, so through the willing obedience of the one man many of us will be made right. When the law came into the picture, sin grew and grew; but wherever sin grew and spread, God's grace was there in fuller, greater measure. No matter how much sin crept in, there

103

was always more grace. In the same way that sin reigned in the sphere of death, now grace reigns through God's *restorative justice*, eclipsing death and leading to eternal life through the Anointed One, Jesus our Lord, the Liberating King" (Romans 5:18-21, emphasis added).

In the biblical context, we see that God's righteousness is not a vengeful moral perfection bent on punishing all those who fail to measure up, unleashing mayhem upon the one who commits the slightest infraction. Chris Seay is helpful here, too: "The best simple translation of the word righteousness is 'restorative justice.' God is stepping into our brokenness and making things right, taking fragments shattered by sin and restoring them to fullness... What was and remains broken in this world because of the fall can be made whole. It can be set right."[10]

The gospel is the good news that the prodigal God's grace eclipses the trend towards destruction and deterioration in which we are all caught up as broken people. The life, death, and resurrection of Jesus has kick-started a new trend, the reign of God's restorative justice, counteracting the old direction. The invitation is to join in that new trend - to find his forgiveness and love that subverts the old way and sets us on a path to becoming truly human. The invitation is to believe him, to trust him, to be restored in relationship with him.

Moreover, to *join him* in restoring all things.

This invitation is available to all. There's hope for everyone. Even if your last name is Phelps. *Or Morgan.*

The choice really is yours.

For those who refuse this invitation and commit to the trend towards destruction and death, in larger or smaller ways, God's justice will be sufficient to deal with that too. He is impartial and fair. He will judge each person according to their deeds.

"As it goes, everyone will receive what his actions in life have cultivated. Whoever has labored diligently and patiently to do what is right - seeking glory, honor, and immortality - God will grant him endless joy in life eternal. But selfish individuals who make trouble, resist the truth, or sell out to wickedness will meet a very different fate - they will find fury and indignation as the fruit of living in the wrong. Suffering and pain await everyone whose life is marked by evil living (first for the Jew, and next for the non-Jew). But if you do what is right, you will receive glory, admiration, and peace (again, first for the Jew, then for the non-Jew). God has no favorites" (Romans 2:6-11).

Dexter Morgan is out for blood. While God's universally vengeful stunt double may emulate Dexter's addiction in the extreme, there is yet something about Dexter's retributive justice that resonates with the real God. That is, Dexter's increasingly relational brand of retribution serves as a helpful illustration of an aspect of God's own justice. In this, Dexter is rightly seen as a hero. Something deep within us knows that a kind of retributive justice is necessary and right. Something deep within God's divine nature requires it. The gospel cannot overlook it.

However, as an illustration of us all, Dexter Morgan's vengeful addiction is yet an outworking of his brokenness. His symbolic box of blood-stained-glass slides is full, but he remains empty. He is only beginning to grasp the greater restorative purpose of the justice for which he is reaching. He remains a broken person, like all of us, on a journey of reconciling the fragments of his flawed humanity.

Restoration supersedes retribution in defining what true justice is. The question becomes, How can we forgive?

"Again, my loved ones, do not seek revenge; instead, allow God's wrath to make sure justice is served. Turn it over to Him. For the Scriptures say, 'Revenge is Mine. I will settle all scores'" (Romans 12:19).

Turn it over to him.

All will stand before a just God.

Blood is All over the atonement

5

A Believer Called Dexter

Don't let me drift too far,
Keep me where you are,
Where I will always be renewed.
And that which you've given me today
Is worth more than I can pay,
And no matter what they say,
I still believe in you.

- BOB DYLAN

There was one problem, however.

Alcohol.

In the early days of drug rehabilitation, alcohol was not really on the radar. It was placed in a different category of vice. My dad recounts how patients in drug rehab would get drink vouchers for good behavior. That night in Clewiston, alone and missing my mom in a cheap motel room, he started drinking. Hard.

It had been raining a while when he got into his Datsun 260z (a token of his success) and began driving. He was more drunk than he realized. My dad has told this story to me so many times, it plays like a movie in my mind: pushing the pedal to the floor to see how fast the car would go, feeling the traction leave and entering a hydroplaning spin, then flipping three or four or five times off the highway and down a grassy embankment until coming to a crashing halt.

He doesn't remember much of what happened at the bottom of the hill, but he does remember that he couldn't move his body. There was no feeling. He does remember seeing fire. He does remember knowing that he was going to die.

He doesn't remember who pulled him out of the car, or how. He has never seen that person since. His next clear memory was in the emergency room, head and body strapped to a gurney, attended to by medical personnel trying to ascertain the extent of his back and neck trauma. And he remembers a conversation.

With God.

The God that my mom believed in and claimed to have a "personal relationship" with. (My dad used to mock her: "So you have an imaginary friend. I have *real* friends.")

Specifically, God in the person of Jesus Christ.

"God, if you will get me out of this," he said, aloud, "I will believe in you. I will serve you. I will dedicate the rest of my life to you."

It may not be an uncommon prayer in such a situation. What is uncommon is the *response*. My dad did not hear something audibly (because that would be strange), but he felt something intensely. A voice within. A knowing deep in his bones. A word, not from his own thoughts, but from somewhere else entirely.

No.

And then: *Believe in me anyway.*

My dad said, aloud, "Yes, I believe."

He has not had a drink since.

Dexter Morgan is a broken man.

By becoming a father, he begins to be restored.

Yet, he is out for blood.

There seems to be a pathway of recovery for Dexter, a restorative road going in the direction of becoming truly human, but we keep watching and waiting as the dismembered bodies pile up. Who will be next, and why? Will there be something different about the next kill? Will it ever change?

Will it ever…end?

We have explored the inner contradiction that embattles Dexter, his Dark Passenger alternately stronger or weaker than his light - but always there, lurking, regardless. However, we have not really explored Dexter's *emptiness*. His hollowness. The space inside him where something should be but is not, something that seems to have been "surgically removed." In the words of one musician, Dexter Morgan is a shell - just a shell.

What, exactly, is missing?

Could it be the same thing that was missing in my dad when he began drinking that night?

As we have seen, Dexter makes no bones about his emphatic agnosticism. If I were an atheist, I'd probably claim Dexter as a faithful mascot (if I wanted a serial killer for a mascot), looking at his unemotional logic as an ideal model for debunking all of those passion-clouded, religious zealots. However, as a believer myself, I simply refuse to ascribe absolute unbelief to our protagonist. That is a subjective judgment, but it is not an unfounded one. Despite his strong claims (including the claim still reverberating out of Season Six's final kill room: "God has nothing to do with this!"), Dexter is, at most, unsure about the divine. This makes perfect sense. A man who struggles to feel *anything* would no doubt fail at feeling the *transcendent*, though he may aspire to do so.

But there are traces of divine activity throughout Dexter's story. Generally, Dexter is on a quest to feel. Most of the time, he does not believe that he can, but he desperately wants to. He aspires to believe. In Season One, Episode Seven, Dexter confronts a teenage killer named Jeremy Downs who reminds him of himself at a young age - except Jeremy has killed innocent people and shows signs that he will kill again. Despite his young age (19) and striking resemblance to Dex, he is in Dexter's crosshairs as the next righteous kill. Miami Metro gets to him first.

In a private interrogation session back at the station, Dexter and Jeremy find a connection:

> **DEXTER:** *I told you, I warned you, don't kill anyone who doesn't deserve to die. Why did you do it?*

> **JEREMY:** *To feel something different.*

> **DEXTER:** *Different than what? What do you normally feel?*

> **JEREMY:** *Nothing. F****ing nothing at all! I hate every… second of it. I can't stand it. Living my life in my head.*

> **DEXTER:** *Does killing make it better?*

> **JEREMY:** *No. Worse…worse than ever.*

115

DEXTER: *I'm a lot like you, you know.*

JEREMY: *Yeah, right. You're a killer?*

DEXTER: *I'm empty. But I found a way to make it feel less…bottomless.*

JEREMY: *How?*

DEXTER: *Pretend. You pretend the feelings are there, for the world, for the people around you. Who knows, maybe one day they will be.*

This revealing exchange sets a trajectory for Dexter's quest to feel. For Dexter, pretense, itself, is actually a form of belief. A leap of faith. A step towards wholeness. His pretense brings the first fruits of feeling "less bottomless."

Clearly, this does not directly pertain to a belief in God, but what could be more transcendent than human connection for a dissocial psychopath? Perhaps seeing the world through Dexter's eyes reveals how divine, how miraculous, love truly is. Relational restoration is a sign and a wonder.

There are, however, *direct* references to God throughout the series. While many of those references seem to deal with the question of divine providence or predestination (e.g., Trinity's kill room assertion: "This isn't your doing; this is God's plan!"), there are more subtle, powerful strokes. None more powerful, perhaps, than the introduction of Brother Sam, played by Mos Def, in Season Six.

Sam is a man with a dark past. We quickly learn that it is quite similar to Dexter's past. Like Dexter, he witnessed a murder up close and personal as a child. Like Dexter, he went on to act out his childhood trauma by committing murder himself. In fact, after bludgeoning a store clerk to death with a bottle, Sam was arrested and imprisoned.

Then something happened.

Divine intervention.

In prison, Sam dragged another man into the chapel and began to strangle him. Brilliant light suddenly shined through the stained glass, straight into Sam's soul, and he saw clearly that his life up to that moment had been all wrong. He let the man go, let him live, knowing it was the best thing he had ever done. Then an unexpected chain of events led to Sam's parole and release from prison. He believed this to be God's doing - the beginning of a calling.

Dexter meets him in the context of his new life's mission - operating a body shop that is really a haven for the offscouring of society. Shepherding a flock of criminals, rejects, and strays. Taking on a new name for this new life: *Brother Sam.*

A "good shepherd."

Brother Sam reminds me of my father.

There is no more famous biblical example of "conversion" than that of Saul.

Saul, who would take on a new name for his new life - *Apostle Paul* - was a nasty character, to say the very least. In his own words, "Jesus the Anointed, the Liberating King, came into the world to save sinners, and I am the worst of them all" (1 Timothy 1:15). *Worst*, meaning an employee of the Jerusalem Temple commissioned to track down the members of a new Jewish sect - men, women, children - and have them imprisoned or executed. His job was to directly oppose God's new action, his new cause, in the world. Saul facilitated the execution of this sect's first martyr, Stephen, who, in the style of his rabbi, prayed that his killers be forgiven as they hurled stones at his head.

"Then he knelt in prayer, shouting at the top of his lungs, 'Lord, do not hold this evil against them!' Those were his final words; then he fell asleep in death" (Acts 8:60).

The new Jewish sect had formed around the life and teaching of a man called Jesus, whom his followers claimed was the Messiah, the liberating Israelite King foretold in the Hebrew scriptures. It was not uncommon in those days for sects like this to form around similar "messiahs" who claimed that they had come to set Israel free from Roman oppression and end the Temple's desecration and abuse - to set up a new Israelite kingdom, the kingdom of God, on earth. The only problem was that these messiahs generally resorted to violent resistance to the political authorities, and were promptly put down or killed by those authorities. The Romans simply had superior firepower.

After the dust settled, the sect would scatter, usually in fear for their lives.

And that would be the end of it.

This is precisely what happened to the Jewish sect that had formed around Jesus when he finally fell victim to the peace-keeping iron fist of the Roman Empire. Convicted in a kangaroo court by the compromised religious elite, then sentenced by an ill-informed mob presided over by the cowardly Pontius Pilate, Jesus found himself facing the worst kind of execution available in the first century: crucifixion.

In the Caesar's own kill room, all hope was lost.

The followers of this would-be messiah fled in fear for their lives. They spent the next days, a week, in hiding. Then, something happened.

Something that resulted, weeks later, in the Jesus-follower Peter - the most fearful of them all - standing among Jerusalem crowds and Temple officials loudly proclaiming that the true Messiah had indeed come, and he was Jesus of Nazareth. The same Messiah that the religious elite, the mob, and the empire had killed dead. The same Messiah that had set up no political state, overthrown no governor or king.

Something happened.

Something that resulted in this Jewish sect nonviolently resisting the corrupt Temple's order to cease speaking of the dead King and desist forming these subversive communities outside of Temple and

Roman control. They wouldn't stop. Even when subjected to brutal injustices, like stoning, they still wouldn't stop. They wouldn't even yell out curses and epithets like most would-be messiahs when they were finally executed. They just prayed for God to forgive.

Something happened.

And so, Saul, the pious Israelite who saw himself as wielding the sword of God's own vengeance, left the scene of Stephen's execution for Damascus in Syria to round up some more of these subversive, heretical dead-king-followers. Until, riding his horse on the road, he saw a light, blinding light that shined all around him and straight into his soul. He fell off his horse, went blind, and heard a voice.

It was Jesus of Nazareth, the Israelite King. *Very much alive.*

Season Five's storyline picks up on the night of Rita's death at the hands of the Trinity Killer, played by John Lithgow. One of the series' writers sheds light on his vision for the season:

"Dexter's a very particular character. He doesn't feel guilt the way we do, he doesn't feel grief the way we do, but he is feeling the weight of these colossal mistakes. We thought in that context that a kind of atonement would be in order... [Y]ou realize that the Code isn't this set of external rules anymore, that he does have this odd kind of morality that he defends and believes in. 'Don't hurt an innocent': he really violated the most basic part of the Code there in a huge way by not protecting his wife and, in fact, bringing this damage onto her. So that particular part of the Code is very alive for him right now."[1]

The dictionary definition for *atonement* is "reparation for an offense or injury." Simply, it is an act of payment that makes a wrong right. A settling of accounts. A reconciling transaction.

The theological idea of atonement occupies the center of Christian faith and is summed up in the symbol of the cross. Believers express this in different ways: "Jesus died for my sins," "He died in my place and took my punishment," "He paid my debt and set me free," "He ransomed my soul from death," etc. In almost every case, the main idea is a substitutionary transaction - he died my death in my place to pay the debt my sins have racked up, giving me his moral righteousness and eternal life in a great exchange.

The goal in all of this is what Christians call *salvation* - to be rescued from the guilt and consequences of my sin, to receive a righteous status and a pardon from the final Judge.

This idea is not new.

"You see, the life of the body is in the blood, and I have directed that you are to take blood and offer it on the altar to atone for your lives and cover your sins. It is the life flowing in the blood that atones for you and covers you" (Leviticus 17:11).

The principle of substitution reaches back to the animal sacrifices of the Mosaic law and culminates in the final sacrifice of Jesus, the Messiah, God's Son. It is a blood-substitution. Blood is all over the atonement.

And atonement is all over *Dexter*. At a fundamental level, Dexter is himself a maker of atonement, ensuring that the just price for sin is paid, blood for blood, settling accounts and making the wrong right. Specifically, he ensures that *others* pay the just price for *their* sins, wrapped in plastic and duct tape and lying flat in his kill room.

However, Season Five represents a slight departure from this theme.

Now, Dexter is the sinner.

Here's how his transgression unfolded. In Season Four, he tragically broke his own inner Code by not killing Arthur Mitchell, the Trinity Killer, when he first had the chance. In the process of stalking Trinity, Dexter had begun a relationship with the friendly alter-ego Arthur Mitchell, a relationship that became a friendship. In fact, Dexter began to view him as a mentor of sorts. His dark admiration for the old psychopath got the better of him, and he let a guilty serial killer live too long, passing up several chances to end Mitchell's life (or let him end his own). Before Dexter finally got him into the kill room, Trinity already had attacked Dexter's beloved wife Rita in her own bathtub, brutally severing her femoral artery and leaving her to bleed out.

"It's already over," said Trinity, on Dexter's table.

With this lethal failure now hanging over Dexter's head, the question becomes, who will be the blood-substitute? Dexter has sinned, aiding and abetting the murder of an innocent. Someone must die in his place, to redeem him. Thus, Season Five opens with a visceral attempt at atonement, however misdirected. A passionate breach of Code. And the sacrifice couldn't be bloodier.

Dexter is on a boat excursion to escape the confusion of family and coworkers in crisis after Rita's death. Daydreaming, he relives a sweet conversation with Rita after their first date. He says, aloud, "Goodbye." And, "I'm sorry." Then he runs out of gas.

He stops, refuels, and goes into the boathouse to pay. There is no clerk. There is only an impatient customer yelling and swearing. The haggard, vile man intentionally bumps Dexter and needlessly insults him. Dexter follows him into the restroom, drawing out more insults from the man, including a wicked insult aimed at the late Rita. There is no proof that this man is a killer, but he at least appears to deserve some kind of punishment.

In this moment of pain, that is all the proof Dexter needs.

Grabbing the small anchor attached to the bathroom key, Dexter approaches the man. "I never meant to hurt her," he says. Then, he attacks, head-butting the man, driving him through the stall door, tackling him to the ground. Taking the anchor in one hand, he begins to swing over and over and over.

After hacking at the body with the sharp edges of the anchor ten times, Dexter finally stops, his own body spattered and soaked with the blood of his victim - literally, "the blood that atones for you and covers you."

Dexter Morgan is, after all, out for blood.

And blood is all over the atonement.

One is reminded of the old hymn:

123

Nothing can for sin atone,
Nothing but the blood of Jesus.
Not a good that I have done,
Nothing but the blood of Jesus.

There is, however, more to atonement than mere spatter.

There are richer hues, blood-red as they may be.

For centuries, the theology of the atonement has been extracted from one primary source: the letters (epistles) of Paul (formerly, Saul), especially the letter to the Romans. It is there that we find this maxim: "[W]hile we were wasting our lives in sin, God revealed His powerful love to us in a tangible display - the Anointed One died for us. As a result, the blood of Jesus has made us right with God..." (Romans 5:8-9).

Thus, for centuries, the theology of the atonement has honed in on one main thing: substitution, the "great exchange" of my moral guilt and death for Jesus' moral righteousness and life. The problem, the only problem, that this atonement theology aims to solve is the problem of individual moral guilt, and the condemnation (death and hell) that results. Jesus died for my sin, so I can be saved from death and hell and go to heaven.

However, atonement does not exist in a theological vacuum. It is part of a much larger narrative. The narrative we have been looking at for four chapters, the narrative that begins in the lush, primordial Garden and ends in the fully restored City, with all the missional work of rescuing broken people and a broken creation in between. The cross, and the atonement, are at the center of that story. Mount Calvary is there, the mountain of law behind it, the final restoration of all things in front of it.

And right in the middle of it all, spattering, streaking, pouring, pooling, is *the blood.*

The blood of Jesus.

What can wash away my sin?
Nothing but the blood of Jesus.
What can make me whole again?
Nothing but the blood of Jesus.

This verse of the hymn hints at the wonderful "more" of the bloody atonement. Namely, it is not merely the pardoning of individual moral guilt that is effected by the blood of Jesus, but the bringing of *wholeness* to the broken person and, by extension, the broken world. This is more than a theological subtlety - this is an emphasis that makes all the difference if, indeed, "God is in the details."

For Saul, the blood was powerful. The cross of Jesus effected a change in him for the benefit of others, of the world. It addressed a problem much bigger than individual, moral guilt or an especially hot afterlife.

Anabaptist theologian John Howard Yoder argues for this larger understanding of atonement and salvation. He sees the righteousness that comes through the Messiah's sacrifice as having fundamentally "cosmic or social dimensions." He writes, "Such larger dimensions would not negate the personal character...but by

125

englobing the personal salvation in a fuller reality they would negate the individualism with which we understand such reconciliation."[2]

Let me be clear: Jesus died on the cross for my sins. His blood washes away my failures, every one. *I believe this.*

Yet, to stop at this individual transaction would rob the blood of its real force. This is about something much bigger than *me*. The blood answers the problem of a world spinning out of control, a world that must be set right again. The blood is cosmic. The cross, the atonement, the blood-substitution creates not just a morally reconciled individual, but a fully reconciled *people* who join God in his mission to reconcile everything.

"God was pleased that all His fullness should forever dwell in the Son who, as predetermined by God, bled peace into the world by His death on the cross as God's means of reconciling to Himself the whole creation - all things in heaven and all things on earth" (Colossians 1:19-20).

The blood of Jesus is a powerful, creative force, not a morbid, unseemly judgment. In this great act of atonement, the Messiah, God's Son and second self, takes on the full weight of humanity's destructive independence in a single crescendo-like moment, stopping the deterioration of creation *dead in its tracks* by fully identifying with us and taking on all our injustice. The cross is, thus, the sublime mingling of justice and grace, God's own body mysteriously broken with all the brokenness of the world, the Son mysteriously absorbing the Father's own anger and disapproval over how things have transpired, ushering in radical forgiveness for broken people and unleashing the spiritual power for healing and right-making. Jesus contained "all the fullness" of God, and, in that moment - a beautiful irony - he also contained all the fullness of sin. The result is a thunderous collision of worlds, rending the division between earth and heaven, launching an entirely new creation on a new life's mission of setting the world right again.

This tangible display of God's love in the blood of the Son takes the tangible shape of a reconciled and reconciling people. A community with a cause. The Apostle Paul calls it the "new humanity."

"His desire was to create in His body one new humanity from the two opposing groups, thus creating peace. Effectively, the cross becomes God's means to kill off the hostility once and for all so that He is able to reconcile them both to God in this one new body" (Ephesians 2:15-16).

This brings us back to the conversion of that man Saul who would become the Apostle Paul. Yoder comments: "What is now set right in his life is not that he has overcome his inner resistances and has become able to trust in God for his right [moral] status before God; it is rather that through the inexplicable intervention of God on the Damascus Road and in later experiences, Paul has become *the agent of the action of God for the right cause*" (emphasis added).[3]

And what is that right cause? "[T]he work of Christ, the making of peace, the breaking down of the wall, is itself the constituting of a new community made up of two kinds of people, those who had lived under the law and those who had not."[4]

The blood is a powerful, creative force. It brings groups together that would otherwise be at odds and reconstitutes them as a new

127

community oriented around the causes of peace, reconciliation, and restorative justice in the neighborhood and the world.

"When God set Him up to be the sacrifice - the seat of mercy where sins are atoned through faith - His blood became the demonstration of God's own restorative justice" (Romans 3:25).

There is, truly, "power in the blood."

Brother Sam is a good shepherd of a new community, a community of broken people who have not "lived under the law." Sam firmly believes they can be restored. For a moment in Season Six, Dexter, who has at least lived under *the Code*, becomes a part of that community of restoration. He even attends a baptism at the beach for an ex-convict named Nick, a member of Sam's flock.

You'd think science would have made religion obsolete...but it hasn't. Go for a swim, come out a new man. If only I believed it were that simple. But Brother Sam believes, and because of that he is fulfilled. It's written all over his face.

SAM: *So what did you think?*

DEXTER: *Ah...interesting. Don't get me wrong, the spiritual stuff, the second chances, I think it's great. For Nick.*

SAM: *But not for you, huh. I get it. But you know, it's not about the dunk, it's about surrender to something greater than yourself.*

Sam embodies a message of "surrender to something greater than yourself." Really, it is a message of filling up the emptiness, of satisfying the deep longing for something beyond this broken world, beyond our broken selves. Dexter is at least aware of his emptiness, even though he doesn't *think* he believes in anything. In Season Six, Episode One, Deb asks him directly:

DEB: *You really believe in nothing?*

DEXTER: *I suppose I believe in a certain set of principles.*

DEB: *What kind of principles?*

DEXTER: *A set of rules on how I conduct myself in the world so I don't get into trouble.*

DEB: *Seriously? "A set of rules to follow so I don't get into trouble"? Sounds like something I might teach a puppy. Sounds kind of cold and empty.*

That's why we are surprised in Episode Five when circumstances push Dexter closer to belief than he's ever been. Dexter's little child, Harrison, suffers a ruptured appendix and is rushed to the hospital; the situation is critical. Dexter is deeply troubled, perhaps more so than at any other time in the series. Sam arrives and urges Dexter, "Sometimes you just gotta surrender."

129

Minutes later, Dexter walks to a Nescafé machine to get coffee. It eats his money. He bumps the machine. Reaching the limit of his patience, he jolts it again, then hangs his head while leaning against it. His next words take the shape of a prayer:

"Come on. Just let him be okay, please let him be okay. I don't know how this works, but if there's something I need to do in return, I'll do it."

Then he raises his voice: "Okay?!"

A cup suddenly drops and the coffee dispenses.

Later we learn that the surgery is successful and Harrison fully recovers.

In the first episode of Season Five, Dexter seeks to atone by punishing another. He is washed in another man's blood. He is still empty.

Not just payment but power is needed. Not just reparation but restoration. Enter: Lumen Pierce.

The atonement storyline takes an interesting turn as Dexter rescues a woman named Lumen. She is the victim of multiple rapes and attempted murder at the hands of a gang of killers. Once rescued, Lumen is hell-bent on revenge; she is out for blood. And in the midst of her trauma, Dexter sees an opportunity to atone for his sin against Rita. By helping Lumen track and put down her attackers, he may be able to make right what had gone terribly wrong.

Dexter and Lumen are successful. They pinpoint the gang's leader Jordan Chase, a motivational speaker by day, sado-masochistic killer by night. Together, they end his dark double life. Dexter even begins to see a future in this vigilante partnership with Lumen - a future fueled by the love that is growing between them. Yet, once Lumen thrusts the knife into Jordan's chest, a sudden change occurs.

She doesn't want to kill anymore. The thirst for vengeance is gone. There is closure; she is becoming whole again.

Here we realize that Dexter is no longer just the sinner trying to right his own wrong. He has himself become the sacrificial lamb. He atoned for Lumen's emptiness, bringing restoration. In tears, Dexter says to Lumen, "Don't be sorry your darkness is gone. I'll carry it for you."

Brother Sam baptized his new convert, Nick, that day at the beach. Dexter was there and an impact was made. He even prayed during a time of crisis.

Yet, as Season Six continues, Brother Sam gets shot.

By Nick.

Sam is murdered by his own disciple, a veritable Judas Iscariot. We watch as Dexter struggles to make sense of a God who would fail to protect such a faithful believer. Against the backdrop of Miami Metro's religion-charged hunt for the Doomsday Killer, Dexter's apparent unbelief is at an all-time high. Now, all he wants is more blood.

He furiously drowns Nick and sets his sights on the next target: Doomsday.

Like the Trinity Killer before him, Travis Marshall, the Doomsday Killer, doesn't disappoint when it comes to God-talk on Dexter's table. In the final kill room, Dexter confronts Travis's faith-based insanity: "I've known people who believed in God. They would never use their faith as a convenient excuse to kill ten people. You used God, not the other way around."

Then a conversation erupts:

> **TRAVIS:** *You're wrong about everything because you don't believe in God. But I have faith, I trust in God's plan.*
>
> **DEXTER:** *Really? Then it must be God's plan that you are on my table. You think it's God's will that I'm about to kill you? God has nothing to do with this! You are wrapped in plastic because I want to kill you.*
>
> **TRAVIS:** *This is not how it's supposed to be!*
>
> **DEXTER:** *Maybe it's exactly as it's supposed to be. Maybe everything is exactly as it should be.*

"Everything is exactly as it should be." An interesting admission from a man who believes in nothing. A sign, however faint, of surrender.

If you ask my dad today, he will tell you that, actually, alcohol was not his problem.

Drugs weren't, either.

The problem was the emptiness.

The problem was the hollowness.

The problem was something that was missing, something that felt as if it had been surgically removed.

The God-shaped hole.

That night in 1977, my father, like Sam and like Saul, found himself suddenly, unexpectedly filled up.

Lying on a gurney, back broken with no promise of physical recovery, he felt joy.

And peace.

Unspeakable peace.

The pain of his desperate failure - his destructive independence that made him at once a mocker of his wife's God and a hypocrite to his own vocation and community - was totally and completely gone.

What can wash away my sin?
Nothing but the blood of Jesus.
What can make me whole again?
Nothing but the blood of Jesus.

Someone had already carried my dad's darkness for him. Someone

133

had already taken my dad's pain, and the pain of the whole world, on himself. Someone was already making my dad, and the whole world, new again.

The Messiah, Jesus.

My father, like Sam and like Saul, drank deeply and found himself filled: "This cup is the new covenant in my blood, which is poured out for you" (Luke 22:20, NIV).

And, like Harrison, he would recover from all of his injuries.

Something happened.

Saul became the Apostle Paul, "the agent of the action of God for the right cause."

The blood of atonement was also the blood of a falsely accused leader from an oppressed Middle-Eastern people group in the first century. The cross of Christianity was also the execution stake of a nonviolent resister to a corrupt religious system and an oppressive empire. The tomb of the murdered Messiah was, and is, *empty*.

Something happened.

Atonement is, thus, more than a spiritual transaction that fixes a problem of individual moral guilt.

Atonement is a community and a cause with the power to change us and the world.

Nothing else can do that.

Nothing but the blood of Jesus.

That's the gospel.

the
Gospel
is
nothing
less than
Real

6

A Community Called Dexter

*"If God raised Jesus Christ from the dead,
everything else is basically rock n' roll, isn't it?"*

- LONDON CABBIE TO N.T. WRIGHT

Three years ago, a group of friends and I chose to acknowledge what we felt was already true - that our living-room experience of worship, study, prayer, and encouragement had become *church* for us. We decided to plant our small community as a new church called Dwell[1], doing life and mission in the least religious city in the least religious state in the US: Burlington, Vermont.

For nearly two years before that, we were simply a group of friends, eight or ten people in all, who loved doing life together. Because we were Christians, we also enjoyed growing spiritually together, encouraging and challenging each other in our faith. And because we were passionate about the gospel of Jesus, we naturally wanted to invite our friends and neighbors into that experience, the experience of Christian community. (Actually, we wanted our whole city to be transformed by it!) It never felt like we were marketing or selling; we were just living life and overflowing. It was the most real experience of Christian life that any of us had ever had up to that point.

As we moved intentionally into the phase of planting and growing Dwell, the task was to create a vision, a structure, and a culture that can reach more people than just our initial eight or ten, all while maintaining - and increasing - the life and energy of those early days. It's a tension we live in daily, and it's a tension we have to embrace because that is where the *realness* is. nd if we know anything about religion, even Christian religion, we know it has ndency to become rather *fake*.

139

The question is, What does authenticity really entail when it comes to living out our faith in community with others?

In 2011, our church went through several difficult trials, including the untimely death of a precious friend and the angry departure of a new member. How do these things confirm or deny the legitimacy of a community of faith? Can it still be real when it's not all roses?

In the preceding chapters, we have surveyed several of the facets of a fictional, yet compelling, man called Dexter. Those facets have, in turn, helped to shed light on several of the facets of the Christian gospel. And who would have thought? The serial killer who kills killers somehow tells us a great deal about our own experience as broken people hoping to be restored, hoping to be made truly human again, hoping for the world to be set right again. That fundamental experience - common, I believe, to all people - is exactly what the good news of Jesus the Messiah is all about.

We have seen that the biblical narrative, even more than Dexter's, is a narrative of *restoration*, stretching from the Garden in Genesis to the City in Revelation. We have seen that the love of God, even more than Harry's love, is his scandalous belief in us, that we can actually live into our true human potential as his Eikons, the image-bearers of God himself. We have seen that the justice of God, even more than Dexter's justice, is his passionate determination to set the world right again, to stop it from spinning completely out of control. We have seen that all of life, even more than all of Dexter's life, is relational - that, if our problem is going to be solved, then it is going to be through healed relationships in every direction. And we have seen that the atonement at the center of the gospel of Jesus, more than any atonement that Dexter can make, has the power to make us - and everything - whole again.

In all of this, there is a contrast with those other "gospels" that seem all too close and those other versions of "God" that show up from time to time as his often (and sometimes, wildly) inaccurate stunt doubles.

Yet, all this gospel-talk would be "much ado about nothing" unless it produced something *real*.

Our community of faith in Burlington was initially inspired in part by Scot McKnight's concise book, *A Community Called Atonement*. Even the chapter titles in the present book are a respectful nod to his work. McKnight sets the tone:

"[T]he gospel itself is an ecclesial, atoning work: it works to create a community in which cracked Eikons are healed in their relations with God, self, others, and the world. Herein lies the telic heart of atonement: *God provides atonement in order to create a fellowship of persons who love God and love others, who find healing for the self, and who care about the world.*"[2]

The gospel creates a community called atonement. In other words, through the community of faith, the good news of restoration and reconciliation is made *real*.

According to recent reports, *Dexter* has been renewed for two more seasons - Seven and Eight.

After Season Eight, Episode Twelve, the television story will be complete.

Season Four is, thus, the lynchpin upon which Dexter's TV story turns. It is the midway point, complete with an "everything changes" kind of moment: the death of Rita Bennett. Season Five opens in the chaotic aftermath of Dexter's tragic mistake, with much atoning drama to follow leading up to Lumen's salvation. But before all that, in Season Five, Episode One, there is a funeral scene in which Dexter says the following words about his murdered wife:

"She had a big heart. Big enough for both of us. Had to be. Because I wasn't even human, when we first met. I never expected that to change, but she reached out and found something I didn't even know was there. She never hurt anybody. She was innocent. And she died a brutal death, and I can't fix it. But I know I have to try, here in Miami with the people who knew her, who cared about her, and who loved her..."

The audio switches to Dexter's narration:

Like I did.

Debra Morgan has a foul mouth.

Really, really foul.

In one episode, Deb weaves together an inexplicably obscene phrase involving R-rated swear words and several religious references (all not repeatable here), to which Dexter can only respond, "I think you might have broken a commandment somewhere in there."

It's kind of her thing.

The full-blooded daughter of Harry Morgan, whom she idolizes, and stepsister to Dexter, Deb is the extra-tough, extra-talented detective that can't seem to catch a break in the Miami Metro Police Department or in her personal life. This is why we viewers love her. She is perpetually tortured by emotional and ethical drama on and off the job, which reminds us of our stressed-out selves. The way she handles the difficulties in her life, through obscenity-laced explosions amidst courageous relational and career risks, smacks of authenticity.

When we watch Deb onscreen, we get the feeling that we are watching a character who simply doesn't possess the ability to fake anything. She is Dexter's opposite, in that sense. Whereas Dexter is struggling to feel anything real, she cannot feel anything else. One even gets the impression that Jennifer Carpenter, the actress who plays Deb, is not at all unlike her character. That is, Jennifer is so real that she can't fake Deb - who is, in turn, the most genuine character on *Dexter*.

In Seasons Two and Four, Deb demonstrates a curious dysfunction by engaging in a love affair with a much older man - FBI agent Frank Lundy. It is immediately obvious that she sees her father in him - the perfect, stern, seasoned cop - and that is the source of the attraction. But there is more happening here. In Season One, Deb was drawn into a relationship with Rudy Cooper, a charming, good-hearted prosthologist connected to one of her investigations. As it turns out, Rudy was actually Brian Moser, Dexter's blood-brother and the infamous Ice Truck Killer himself, and his motives were sinister: get close to Dexter and kill Deb with his help. She narrowly escapes her own murder.

143

In Season Three, Deb is at it again with Anton Briggs, a confidential informant (CI) for Miami Metro. By dating Anton, she is following in her father's footsteps; Harry slept with his CI's too. That was how Dexter's problems began in the first place: Laura Moser, Dexter's mother, was one of Harry's CI girlfriends. Harry placed her in the perilous situation that resulted in her death at the hands of drug-dealing thugs - a moment, witnessed by the three-year-old Dexter, which became the bloody fountainhead of his dark urge.

In all of this, we see the entanglement of family and community and the potential for destruction, given each person's weaknesses and sins. It all seems to come to a head for Deb in Season Four as her relationship with Lundy is reignited. She cheats on Anton, he leaves her, and she pursues a deeper commitment to the father-figure boyfriend. But then Frank is shot and killed by none other than Christine Hill, the daughter of Arthur Mitchell, the brutal Trinity Killer.

It's a messy situation.

Deb is with Lundy when it happens. She catches a bullet to the hip. Her life comes apart at the seams.

The bitter irony of Deb's unraveling in Season Four is the fact that it all revolves around her greatest passion, the thing that makes her feel most alive - being a cop. All of these relationships are connected to her career; it is as if she is being punished for trying to do what she loves in the shadow of the father she idolizes. The frustration caused by her impossible situation is put on stunning display in a scene from Episode Five. For me, it remains the most powerfully acted scene in the entire series. It may be one of the most powerful scenes in recent TV history.

Dexter and Deb survey the parking lot where Lundy was shot. Deb is distraught, forlorn. She begins to cry, softly at first, but becoming more hysterical with each word. She is breaking down:

> **DEB:** *Yesterday, I had Lundy and Anton. And now they're gone, because of me.*

> **DEXTER:** *You didn't do anything wrong.*

> **DEB:** *It doesn't matter what I do, or what I choose – I'm what's wrong. There's nothing I can do about it. If I'm not hurting myself, I'm hurting everyone around me, there's nothing I can do about it. I…I am broken!*

> **DEXTER:** *No, you're not. I am.*

In a single moment, the truth is laid bare. Dexter is not the only broken person in this story. He may be the most broken, but he is part of a broken community. His words of encouragement for his sister can't erase the pain of that fact. Deb may be too hard on herself, but she is basically right.

Looking at ourselves through Dex and Deb's story, we may say the very same thing: "I'm what's wrong. I am broken."

The scene ends as two broken people, stepbrother and stepsister, embrace.

The central claim of the Christian gospel is this: *the world can be set right again.*

Alongside that stands the powerful implication: *we can become truly human again.*

Rob Bell is spot-on when he writes the following:

"What the gospel does is confront our version of our story with God's version of our story. It is a brutally honest, exuberantly liberating story, and it is good news. It begins with the sure and certain truth that we are loved. That in spite of whatever has gone horribly wrong deep in our hearts and has spread to every corner of the world, in spite of our sins, failures, rebellion, and hard hearts, in spite of what's been done to us or what we've done, God has made peace with us. Done. Complete. As Jesus said, 'It is finished.' We are now invited to live a whole new life..."[3]

The gospel shapes a whole new life based on the powerful love of a prodigal God and the atoning justice of a crucified and risen Messiah. This gospel-shaped life is fundamentally a becoming-truly-human life. It is marked by the mending of our brokenness in every personal dimension (spirit, mind, and body) and every relational direction (with God, self, others, and the world). Far from merely being a story of morally guilty people having their transgressions pardoned, the gospel is the story of relationally broken people being made whole again, and the world along with them.

This is a beautiful idea, but is it a unique idea? At this point, it is natural to ask why and how the Christian gospel *uniquely* shapes a becoming-truly-human life. Aren't there other ways out there to "get there"? Certainly, our globalized, pluralistic era offers us a variety of religious and ethical visions, all of which may benefit one in the journey of seeing that which is broken within them and around them restored. So isn't it really up to the individual to choose which vision works best for them?

In Chapter Three, we briefly looked at the event that follows on the heels of the atonement, the cross, the blood: namely, the resurrection. It is crucial to note that according to the Apostle Paul, the resurrection is the key ingredient in the whole gospel recipe, so much so that without it, the gospel is sufficiently powerless and we are all sufficiently hopeless. Here are his words:

"Friends, if the Anointed has not been raised from the dead, then your faith is worth less than yesterday's garbage, you are all doomed in your sins, and all the dearly departed who trusted in His liberation are left decaying in the ground. If what we have hoped for in the Anointed doesn't take us beyond this life, then we are world-class fools, deserving everyone's pity" (1 Corinthians 15:16-19).

Since the beginning of the Christian movement, it has been a staple of orthodoxy to confess "the resurrection of the body, and the life everlasting" - the body, in this case, not referring to Jesus' body but the bodies of all people who have died in faith. But the specifics of this were muddied over the centuries as a vague idea of "heaven" took hold of the popular imagination. For the most part, Christians advanced this idea that the goal of one's earthly life is to "get saved" from what is coming in the afterlife, namely, a *disembodied hell* of torture and torment. In turn, the goal is to reside eternally in a *disembodied heaven* of felicity and bliss. Thus, Christian evangelism has largely become the awkward act of "soul-winning" - one

147

person convincing another person to make a primarily intellectual transaction (believe in Jesus, receive forgiveness and eternal life) that will secure their soul's residence in a glowing celestial city. As for their body, well, that doesn't really matter. As for this world, well, that doesn't matter, either, as it will all be destroyed by tribulation and judgment in the end (to the degree that working for justice now is akin to polishing the brass on the Titanic).

The Apostle Paul's argument in 1 Corinthians 15 is precisely the opposite - that, in fact, the resurrection of *the body*, beginning with the Messiah's body and continuing with our own bodies, is the *sine qua non* of Christian hope. If Christ was not raised from death, and if we will not be raised from death, then this whole thing is one big, terrible joke. His logic is stunning: "Look at it this way: through Adam all of us die, but through the Anointed One all of us can live again. But this is how it will happen: the Anointed's awakening is the firstfruits. It will be followed by the resurrection of all those who belong to Him at His coming, and then the end will come" (verses 22-24).

It is about *this body*, and it is about *this world*: "Then, when all creation has taken its rightful place beneath God's sovereign reign, the Son will follow, subject to the Father who exalted Him over all created things; then God will be God over all" (verse 28). The goal is the restoration of the creation - the earth! - itself, with fully restored, resurrected human beings at the center of it all. Over it all, the Father and the Son.

First and foremost, then, the uniqueness of what the Christian vision is offering us is the certain final restoration of the broken creation.

All will be returned to wholeness, to peace, to perfection, to *shalom*, in the end. Therefore, the life of becoming truly human in Christ is markedly different than all other attempts at "getting there" precisely because there is a certainty of actually "getting there"!

The Christian hope in the "resurrection of the body" is really the continuation of the same Jewish hope, a hope that was palpable in Jesus' own time. First-century Israelites largely believed that the end of the current age would include the resurrection of the dead and deteriorating bodies of "the just" to be vindicated as such by God the Judge, in parallel with the prophetic promise of the restoration of creation. Jesus introduced a present beginning to this ultimate hope. His own resurrection from the dead was the "firstfruits," setting the resurrection/restoration process in motion already. This allowed the Apostle Paul to exclaim: "Therefore, if anyone is in Christ, the new creation has come: The old has gone, the new is here!" (2 Corinthians 5:17, NIV).

The new creation entails an experience of resurrection life now, filling the emptiness and enabling us to begin to become the human beings we were made to be in every dimension of being alive. Jesus' death and resurrection is a now-and-later kind of liberation, an already-and-not-yet kind of salvation, an "it is finished" and "it has just begun" and "just wait until you see what's next" kind of story.

This brings us to still another sense in which the Christian vision is unique: it presents us with an entirely different kind of virtue. NT Wright adds clarity here:

"Some of the greatest minds in the history of Christianity have wrestled with that question, looking at the 'natural human' virtue and the 'specifically Christian' virtue, and have come up with a variety of answers. The key to it all, though, is that the Christian vision of virtue, of character that has become second nature, is precisely all about discovering what it means to be truly human - human in a way most of us never imagine…"[4]

He continues to describe this as becoming "genuine human beings, reflecting the God in whose image we're made" by following Jesus into a new way of life. This "produces, through the work of the Holy Spirit, a transformation of character."[5]

The gospel, the thing that this book is really about, "begins with the sure and certain truth that we are loved." It continues with the invitation and empowerment to live a whole new resurrection-life as part of a whole new creation. It's a life of virtue, a life of transformation, a life of following Jesus, a life of becoming truly human again as we hope in the world being set right again.

Because of that, the Christian gospel is nothing less than *real*.

I'm a very neat monster.

Dexter's dilemma is fundamentally one of identity.

Who is he, really? Is he the Dark Passenger, or is the Dark Passenger merely attached to his true self, along for the ride, vying for attention and prominence, taking the wheel? Is he basically the monster that Harry saw, or is he actually the "good kid" trying to keep the monster at bay by only killing animals?

In the finale episode of Season One, Brian Moser, the Ice Truck Killer, weighs in on this question of identity. He is Dexter's blood-brother, there with him when their mother was murdered. He sat alongside his little brother in the blood of the slain for two days in a stiflingly hot shipping container, suffering the same trauma and emotional scarring that would lead to a hideous urge and a life of taking life. For Brian, ever since that trauma occurred, self-actualization has been the ultimate goal, and there is no restraint - no Code - to stand in the way of that. He addresses Dexter in his kitchen:

"I know what you've been going through all these years - the isolation, the otherness, the hunger that's never satisfied. But you're not alone anymore, Dexter. You can be yourself, with me. Your real, genuine self. Takes the breath away, doesn't it?"

Our sympathies are aroused by this plea until the scene changes to a garage kill room with a special victim sedated on the table: Deb, the stepsister. She was prepared by Brian in Dexter's own style, feet and midsection wrapped to the table by plastic sheeting, head affixed to the table by duct tape. To join Brian in embracing his true identity fully, Dexter need only join him in killing *her*. With this kind of table set for a man who is out for blood in the most visceral sense, the conversation intensifies:

> **BRIAN:** *Tell me something. Your victims – are they all killers?*

> **DEXTER:** *Yes.*

BRIAN: *Harry teach you that?*

DEXTER: *He taught me a Code, to survive.*

BRIAN: *Like an absurd avenger?*

DEXTER: *That's not why I kill.*

BRIAN: *You can be yourself around me. Who am I?*

DEXTER: *A killer. Without reason or regret. You're free.*

BRIAN: *You could be that way too.*

If Dexter's true self is the killer without reason or regret, then everything else in his life, every person, every relationship, is simply part of his disguise. *His mask.* This is often how Dexter views his life. Everything, from a romantic dinner with Rita to a heartfelt talk with Deb to a kill room draped in painter's grade plastic (catching every drop of blood, leaving no trace), are simply props in the facade, protecting and preserving his true, secret self.

His true self is the monster. The neatness is the monster's means of survival.

Dexter seems to repeatedly confront this dilemma when he comes into deeper relationship with various people in his life. Those people may be primary characters in the series, like Deb, Rita, or the kids, but they are often the main antagonists that appear from season to season. Brian Moser. Arthur Mitchell. Lumen Pierce. Lila West. *Miguel Prado.*

Miguel is the main antagonist in Season Three, played flawlessly by Jimmy Smits. He is an unlikely killer, and he only enters the "trade" because of his strange relationship with Dexter. By day, Prado is the Assistant District Attorney for the City of Miami, well-known for his fierce commitment to convicting violent criminals. But his own violent urge is triggered after his drug addict brother, Oscar, is murdered.

That is how Dexter enters the picture. Dexter accidentally killed Oscar in self-defense while hunting Oscar's murderous drug dealer, Freebo. Dexter was stalking Freebo because he had previously killed two college coeds and gotten away with it scot-free. A bad warrant was to blame. In the aftermath of his brother's murder, Miguel assumes that Freebo killed Oscar and begins to hunt him down too. The law failed to bring Freebo to justice the first time, and Miguel does not want to risk that happening again. He is now a vigilante.

Little does he know, Dexter is still hunting.

As luck - or the ingenuity of *Dexter's* writers - would have it, Dexter and Miguel track Freebo to the same hideout on the same night. Dexter brings Freebo into the kill room he set up in the garage. He does the deed. Then he bumps into Miguel outside. Miguel is grateful for Dexter's courage as a vigilante enforcer, bringing his brother's alleged killer to justice.

A friendship is born.

Miguel sees Dexter's Dark Passenger and doesn't look away. In fact, he discovers something about himself - he wants to kill too. Dexter's identity crisis is temporarily resolved in Miguel's own self-actualization, and Dexter is able to take off the mask.

153

With Harry's internal voice warning him against it all the way, Dexter embarks on the kind of close, manly friendship he has witnessed in others but always thought out of reach for himself. With a sly grin and a guy growl, Miguel shouts, "Dex!" and invites him to lunch or nine holes at the country club. Together, they plan the next kill, targeting a violent criminal who has eluded the law, with Harry's Code as their covenant and guide.

It all seems so wonderful, so real.

> Miguel and I took a life together
> and today someone knows my truth.
> Shares my reality. I'm not alone.

Until Dexter discovers that Miguel is just using him as a means to his own twisted ends. Prado learns Dexter's technique and then goes rogue, killing a personal enemy, defense attorney Ellen Wolf. *An innocent woman.* The covenant is broken.

> Too many people are affected when the
> innocent die. That is part of the lesson plan.
> No one is untouchable. I learned that the hard
> way. So will Miguel. His own vulnerability
> is about to become very real to him.

Questions of identity lead to the danger of hypocrisy. Just what does it mean to live an authentic life as your true self? And what does it mean to be part of an authentic community? How does one shed the mask without losing oneself in the process? For Dexter, the frustration comes into play whenever he tries to embrace the monster, the Dark Passenger, as his true self in the presence of another. Brian Moser. Arthur Mitchell. Lumen Pierce. Lila West. *Miguel Prado.*

It just never seems to work out. Now, Miguel, the hypocrite, must die.

> **Today, I keep up the pretense. But soon, maybe tomorrow, Miguel will know exactly how I feel. Because finally there's an emotion I don't have to fake. Today, I feel something real.**

That genuine sense of Christian community that my friends and I experienced in the early days was beautiful in many ways, one of which was the sense of honesty. There was a freedom to be real about the fact that we are broken people who make up a broken community. This was fundamental to our life together.

Truly, a dangerous hypocrisy may set in if that fact is not acknowledged and accepted from the very start. We all have our dark passengers. There is a monster of sorts in each of us. The gospel begins there, with a brutally honest inward look. Yet, the question is still one of identity. As we come to a life of faith in Jesus, who are we really? Where do we locate our true, authentic selves, both individually and collectively?

In a community of faith, it is tempting to answer that question in the way that Dexter often answers it and identify our true self as the monster, the dark passenger, the deeply broken person, the sinner by nature and choice. It is tempting to take a sense of pride in that identity, calling it authentic. Real community.

A real life of faith, we might say, is one in which we identify ourselves primarily, if not exclusively, as broken people, caught in a dissocial spiral of destructive independence, bent and broken bearers of the *imago Dei*, with lives fragmenting in every direction. The goal is to just be honest about it and accept who we really are, together. To take off the mask and not look away, much like Dexter's community of murderous main antagonists - though hopefully with less plastic.

Rick McKinley is pastor of a church called Imago Dei in Portland, Oregon. In a recent sermon, he reflected on the idea of authenticity in Christian community, especially as it pertains to the history of their church. His observation is as humorous as it is powerful:

"In the early days we talked about authentic community at Imago: authentic, authentic, authentic. And we still want to be authentic, authentic, authentic. But then what we found out is that when we were authentic it was like, wow, you're just bitter and angry and complaining a lot. And we never moved past there, and if you tried to move me past there, I'd be like, 'Well, I'm being authentic! You want me to be fake?' It's like, not really, I just want you to quit being a jerk... I don't know that it's God's design to say, 'You're real, now stay there forever.' Get real, but know that [God says], 'I'm going to totally transform you into the image of my Son.' So start honest, I'm not saying don't be honest. But it's dishonest to stay there."[6]

The gospel begins with our brokenness, but it moves on from there to something more. That is the whole point. God's version of our story speaks a different word. He casts another vision. He speaks of a whole new life, a new creation, a new, true identity.

Rick's sermon was mainly drawn from this passage in the book of Acts:

"The community continually committed themselves to learning what the apostles taught them, gathering for fellowship, breaking bread, and praying. Everyone felt a sense of awe because the apostles were doing many signs and wonders among them. There was an intense sense of togetherness among all who believed; they shared all their material possessions in trust. They sold any possessions and goods that did not benefit the community and used the money to help everyone in need. They were unified as they worshiped at the temple day after day. In homes, they broke bread and shared meals with glad and generous hearts. The new disciples praised God, and they enjoyed the goodwill of all the people of the city. Day after day the Lord added to their number everyone who was experiencing liberation" (Acts 2:42-47).

This is the way the Christian movement began, as a brand new expression of community empowered by the life, death, and resurrection of Jesus and the surprising work of the Holy Spirit. Just a glance at this passage reveals that there was commitment, fellowship, togetherness, sharing, unity, gladness, and radical generosity. In other words, there was authentic community, a real experience of Christian life - something we have experienced all throughout the forming, planting, and growing of Dwell.

157

There was something else, too: the people were learning from their leaders (the Apostles) a particular way of looking at the world in light of Jesus the Messiah. They were worshiping God "day after day." All of them were "experiencing liberation," a powerful transformation of character that brought freedom from all kinds of bondage, individually, socially, and even politically.

In other words, this brand new expression of community was authentic in the sense that it was a collective embracing of a particular identity, of a hope, an ideal, a meaning. Under the tutelage of their leaders and amidst the shaping of their worship, it was real in the sense that it was the embracing of an entirely new reality as an entirely new creation.

These early followers of Jesus were coming together to build something: a becoming-truly-human community with a particular vision of the kind of virtue this entails.

In that sense, it was an authentic community precisely because it was starting in honest brokenness while striving to become something better by the power of God. And this is precisely what the real, authentic community of faith must be today. It always has a goal in mind:

"The goal is the new heaven and new earth, with human beings raised from the dead to be the renewed world's rulers and priests... Christian living in the present consists of anticipating this ultimate reality through the Spirit-led, habit-forming, truly human practice of faith, hope, and love, sustaining Christians in their calling to worship God and reflect his glory into the world."

Our young church grew up a bit during the last year and there were growing pains involved. For one, we went through the difficult process of having a recent member leave the church in anger and frustration. This brought on some serious reflection as to what it means to be authentic.

Specifically, it drove us to think about our long-term presence as a church in our city. We began to realize, in the same way that Rick McKinley expressed above, that to be authentic means to hold tightly to the vision of becoming truly human in Christ, over the long haul. This vision begins with the realness of our common brokenness and the way in which we all participate in that dissocial spiral of destructive independence that the whole world is caught up in. However, it doesn't stop there - it calls us up and out into the goal of restored relationships in a fully restored world, and it anticipates that ultimate reality in the here and now.

This means that the Christian community engages in the very real work of both admitting our brokenness and moving forward out of our brokenness through everyday life together. Individually, we realize that our true self is not the first Adam still rebelling inside of us, but the second Adam, Jesus, and his accomplishment outside of us as the truly human being. We accept God's version of our story over and against our own version: that we are accepted, that we are loved, that it is finished, that we are reconciled, that we are already-and-not-yet truly human in the Messiah. And we begin to live into that story.

This kind of life in community implies the possibility that hypocrisy may emerge and be exposed. Some may not want to move forward into something better than the brokenness they are embracing.

159

They may choose to leave a real community, sometimes angrily. The spiral may be too strong, at least for a time. Sometimes, that vortex may even be so strong that it lashes back at the community with gales of frustration, even as it sucks in the person once nurtured there. In such cases, there is great pain, but also great hope. If the house stands as it was built in the way of Jesus and the Apostles, there is a lasting invitation to the city to become truly human, to be made whole again, to join God in setting all things right.

Dexter Morgan is struggling to find a community.

> ## The danger of community is that the people who don't belong are looked upon with suspicion. Those of us who prefer to work by ourselves, the lone wolves, risk being singled out.

The most logical community in which to locate a blood spatter analyst from a famous family of police officers is Miami Metro Homicide. But, Dexter is listless there, too:

> ## Cops. Another community I'm not part of.

Yet, his attempts at finding authentic community with those who seem to be more like him, those who are killers themselves, mostly end with those fellow community members wrapped in plastic, adding samples to his slide collection.

My search for connection always ends in blood.

That is because, deep down, Dexter knows who he is supposed to be.

He has seen his real identity.

It is not the monster.

It is not the Dark Passenger.

It is, instead, the child who lost his mother - and with her, his innocence. It is the boy who wanted nothing more than to please his stepfather. It is the stepbrother who stands over the table, knife in hand, with the urge to kill pulsing through his veins, and yet says to his ruthless blood-brother Brian, "I can't. Not Deb. I'm very...fond of her."

It is the brother who proclaims to the monster, "I am stronger than you."

It is the husband who grieves the wife he loved and promises to make things right.

It is the father who says, yearning:

Maybe I can learn to be better...
A better father to my son...
I want to be a better father...
For Harrison.

Debra Morgan has a foul mouth.

Yet, she is real.

Authentic community calls us to take off the mask of pretense and say with honesty, "It doesn't matter what I do, or what I choose. I'm what's wrong. I am broken." Saying this is not merely for the purpose of revealing brokenness. It is for the purpose of becoming better.

Whole again.

Dex and Deb are broken people. They embrace and there is a community of brokenness. But it doesn't stop there. It doesn't stop there because Dexter wants to become truly human. He feels it with Deb; Rita; Astor and Cody; and, most of all, Harrison.

He feels connection.

Integration.
Belonging.
Wholeness.

Shalom.

Our young church grew up a bit last year and there were growing pains involved.

There is a kind of hypocrisy that acknowledges neither the starting place of brokenness nor the goal of "betterness." It is a sordid indulgence in dark sins while speaking brashly of bright righteousness. An authentic community of faith may experience something like the fury of the hypocrite Miguel Prado, who finally screams in Dexter's face on the roof of the Miami Metro Police building, "I'll do what I want, when I want, to whomever I want - count on it!" This does not deny the community's legitimacy, but confirms it. It is functioning rightly as a becoming-truly-human community - and some would simply rather go in the opposite direction.

The community must press on down the unique path to wholeness, moving forward, always forward. That's where we find our true self. Our real identity.

The Apostle Paul describes it this way:

"They are strangers and aliens to the kind of life God has for them because they live in ignorance and immorality and because their hearts are cold, hard stones... But this is not the path of the Anointed One, which you have learned. If you have heard Jesus and have been taught by Him according to the truth that is in Him, then you know to take off your former way of life, your crumpled old self - that dark blot of a soul corrupted by deceitful desire and lust - to take a fresh breath and to let God renew your attitude and spirit. Then you are ready to put on your new self, modeled after the very likeness of God: truthful, righteous, and holy" (Ephesians 4:18-24).

To those who would angrily reject the work of healing in their lives for a dark and destructive brokenness, these words from post-punk band *Aficionado* are apropos:

Memorize the words, not what they mean,
Although they stand at glaring contradiction
To all the things you say that you believe.

163

You just like the colors, you don't like the team.

And I swear to God sometimes,
You people have no ears,
You have no eyes.[7]

We experienced other growing pains last year too.

Our community suffered a far greater loss. A longtime friend and beloved member of our family of faith lost her year-long battle with breast cancer. She was only 49.

She was like a sister to me.

The injustice of this loss is still almost too much to bear. It is not right. She, of all people, did not deserve this. She was a woman of compassion, selflessness, and virtue - living the kind of life that points to becoming truly human in a way most of us never imagine. She had more to do; her work was not finished.

What does it mean to be an authentic community of faith in a moment like that?

It means to find the only real hope available.

A sure and final hope.

Resurrection.

In the words of *Typhoon*, in a song that we played for her

memorial service:

I promised you I'm never giving up,
Never giving up, never giving up,
I won't give in.
But now that my body's giving up,
My legs are giving out, my head is throwing up its hands,
It's asking:

Can we wait for the summer again?
Can we hold out for summer again?
Will we ever be whole again?

I will wait for the summer,
I will hold out for summer.

There is a promised land
In every man's heart.
There is a summer.[8]

I believe in the resurrection of the body.

And the life everlasting.

There is a summer.

Dexter Morgan Matters

A Politic Called Dexter

*"Run for office? No. I've slept with too many women, I've done
too many drugs, and I've been to too many parties."*

- GEORGE CLOONEY

*"If this is going to be a Christian nation that doesn't help the poor, either
we have to pretend that Jesus was just as selfish as we are, or we've got to
acknowledge that He commanded us to love the poor and serve the needy
without condition and then admit that we just don't want to do it."*

- *Stephen Colbert*

Dexter Morgan
is a broken man.

A member of a broken community.

But he and his community may choose
to embrace a life of becoming truly human.

A life of setting the world right again.

It does not require a great leap of the imagination
to see Dexter as a leader in this community of his,
however *unorthodox* his leadership may be under a
bare, hanging bulb in the kill room. The community
that has formed around his leadership - including
Rita, Deb, the kids, Miami Metro Homicide, the FBI,
and the main antagonists that enter his orbit - is formed,
knowingly or not, for a particular way of life in the world.
Dexter may not run for political office or captain of the police
force (although it would be an interesting plot consideration for
the final two seasons), but he does have *a people* who follow him
and a Constitution he now embodies: Harry's Code, in the flesh.

His community is, in other words, a body politic.

We have seen that Dexter struggles to connect, not least with an actual politician like Miguel Prado. But Miguel is a great case study in Dexter's political presence. It is, first and foremost, a powerful presence - Miguel ends up on Dexter's table even though he claims to control "City f***ing Hall." Secondly, it is a subversive presence - it does not make use of the usual means of power and control in order to set things right. Dexter's politic is that of a Dark Defender, not a District Attorney. His headlines are surprising, unexpected - if there are any headlines at all. He may be in charge, but it is free of selfish corruption. In other words, Dexter is someone the average person may actually *want* in charge.

Because of this, Dexter's politic, his way of forming and shaping his community for life in the world, is one that consistently exposes the inherent hypocrisy of power in its pursuit of justice.

If I may extrapolate from the preceding pages, his presence is one that profoundly recognizes human brokenness (even the brokenness in himself, the leader), and yet unapologetically calls for movement towards restorative justice, setting the world right again, becoming truly human. Just as his community is a becoming-truly-human community, so his politic is a becoming-truly-human politic. In this way, it may even be a model to be emulated (though not, of course, in bloody detail).

In the finale episode of Season One, Dexter entertains the fantasy that he is actually a public figure. He imagines that his recent extermination of the Ice Truck Killer provokes such enthusiasm in the City of Miami that a parade is thrown in his honor, with confetti and signs and adoring fans heralding his arrival to the crime scene. One man says, "Way to take out the trash. Thanks, buddy." A hysterical woman yells, "Alright, Dexter! Protecting our children!" Dexter lifts his hand and smiles in triumph.

He may be darkly dreaming here, but the perspective is crystal clear: Dexter means something to the world he lives in, whether people recognize it or not.

Dexter Morgan matters.

As I write this chapter, our country is in the throes of the Republican presidential primaries, to see who will run against President Obama in November (which is, by the way, about a month after *Dexter* Season Seven will premiere on Showtime).

The Republican primaries have featured an impressive number of televised debates and an even more impressive array of campaign ads. By this time in the race, it is beginning to get heated, if not a bit ugly. But one of the most controversial aspects of this political season has little to do with the candidates' views on social issues or government spending. Instead, it has to do with something called a "Super PAC."

A Super PAC (Political Action Committee) is a fundraising organization that may raise unlimited dollars to be used in promoting and even supporting a particular political campaign, as long as it is not in direct communication with that campaign. In other words, individuals, groups, or corporations that have a vested interest in the policy and platform of a particular candidate can donate to the Super PAC to bypass legal fundraising limitations placed on donations to the campaign itself. Then, the Super

PAC may use those funds for everything from campaign ads to subsidizing travel expenses for candidates. This means that a candidate making policy promises to wealthy people, groups, or corporations can find him or herself swimming in cash from those special interests via the Super PAC. It is a middle-man, a loophole.

Public awareness of Super PAC's spiked when comedic talkshow host Stephen Colbert decided to start one himself in order to openly mock this undemocratic trend. The name of the PAC? "Americans for a Better Tomorrow, Tomorrow."[1]

All of this is especially relevant given the recent emergence of a subversive social movement called Occupy Wall Street (or simply, Occupy). While there is much debate over the coherence and endurance of the movement, it has made an undeniable impact on the culture at every level, calling those in the highest places of power to take notice. Its message is rather simple: there is an unjust economic disparity between the minority of wealthiest Americans and the majority of the population, which gives undue power to individuals and corporations within that minority who influence and direct legislation with their enormous wealth. Everything from tax law to corporate regulation to real estate regulation to foreign policy to *elections* may be influenced by those who occupy the wealthiest minority ("the 1 percent"). So the movement calls the vast majority ("the 99 percent") to "occupy" in return, performing sustained demonstrations in financial and government districts nationally (like Zuccotti Park near Wall Street in New York City), and now even globally.

No matter what your political persuasion, one thing is irrefutable. In the midst of a devastating global recession, voices are crying out for justice and fairness.

John Howard Yoder clarifies the role and scope of Jesus' life and work:

"Jesus was not just a moralist whose teachings had political implications; he was not primarily a teacher of spirituality whose public ministry unfortunately was seen in a political light; he was not just a sacrificial lamb preparing for his immolation, or a God-Man whose divine status calls us to disregard his humanity. Jesus was, in his divinely mandated (i.e., promised, anointed, messianic) prophethood, priesthood, and kingship, the bearer of a new possibility of human, social, and therefore political relationships."[2]

In other words, the impact of Jesus' life cannot be limited to spirituality, morality, or any other one area. The scope of his work is all-encompassing in a relational sense. This includes the social and political areas of life in the world. Jesus came bearing a new possibility of political relationships.

In fact, Jesus' identity as "Christ" is specifically pointing to this political aspect. He came as Israel's promised, anointed Messiah - the Liberating Israelite King. His task was nothing less than the announcement and inauguration of a kingdom.

Jesus was the leader of the community that formed around him. N.T. Wright says, "Throughout his short public career *Jesus spoke and acted as if he was in charge.*" He continues:

"He was the king they'd all been waiting for. If we look for a parallel in today's world, we won't find it so much in the rise of a new 'religious' teacher or leader as in the emergence of a charismatic, dynamic politician whose friends are encouraging him to run for president - and who gives every appearance of having what it takes to sort everything out when he gets there. You might have thought, and people certainly did at the time, that Jesus' untimely death dashed all those hopes once and for all. But not long after his death his associates started to claim that he was now in charge, for real."[3]

If this is true, we must ask how exactly this King and his kingdom may be relevant to our political lives today. Just how should followers of Jesus in 2012 (an election year) function as a body politic in the world? Just how should the Christian community, the church, form itself for life in the world according to a Spirit-authored Constitution, an embodied Code and Covenant? Perhaps most importantly, how should the people of God continue to make the announcement and live out the reality that our leader Jesus is, in fact, in charge?

The political question is even more pressing when we consider the fog that blankets the land, giving us a gospel that is so close, yet so far away. In their extensive study of American opinion about modern-day Christianity, David Kinnaman and Gabe Lyons identified "too political," "judgmental," and "hypocritical" as majority opinions among non-Christian people, especially young people. "At the very least," they write, "we must come to grips with the sheer scope of the issue. The number of young people in our culture who now embrace unflattering perspectives about Christians and politics is astounding. Three-quarters of young outsiders...describe present-day Christianity as 'too involved in politics.'"[4]

This is clearly pointing to the traditional morality platform of the so-called "religious right" that we introduced in Chapter One. The culture has observed a terrible hypocrisy here. People see a supposedly spiritual and moral way of life entangled in the pursuit of excessive amounts of money and power. They see the preaching of salvation in one breath, and the invoking of God's name while declaring war and launching air strikes in the next. They see a party spirit that casts judgment and condemnation on those from other cultural and religious walks of life, while leaders continue to make headlines with scandalous sexual and financial behavior. The "gospel" that waves the banner of traditional morality and vows to fight against the immoral "them" is simply compromised by its own inconsistencies and its glaring lack of the foremost truly human virtue: love.

The answer to this pressing political question, then, is clearly not that the Christian community ought to be more heavily and fiercely devoted to American politics. The answer, rather, is that there is an entirely different type of politic that the church of Jesus is called to express. And we discover the essence of this politic by looking back to the first century. This politic is found in the type of King that Jesus came to be. It is found in the particular *means* through which he was taking charge of the world. And it is found in the sort of Code he was drafting and the community he was creating to embody it.

Jesus was a political leader who was, in fact, forming a body politic around him, a community whose presence would be unbelievably powerful, but in an unexpected, unlikely, and subversive manner.

With love at the center of it all.

By this time, we are well-aware that Dexter Morgan is out for blood.

Blood is the symbol of Dexter's addiction, as well as his art. At one crime scene in the Pilot episode, Dexter recreates the blood spatter trajectory using red string. In the modern white living room, it is beautiful, not unlike a strange exhibition at an art gallery. Dexter elegantly explains his theory on the murder to a cop nearby:

"Look at the blood spatter, look at the patterns. Tells a story. You see that pond of blood right there? That's from the initial stab. The male victim was standing right here, and the killer plunged his knife into the shoulder, severing the carotid artery. And...*splat*. Notice the long heavy drips? Now, over here you have nice, clean sprays of blood. And that can only happen when you're holding something light and moving quick. Nice, sharp slices through the body, no splashes, no drips. Clean and easy. This guy knew how to use a blade."

And so does Dexter.

We have seen that Dexter's way of vengeance, though shocking, may at least help to illustrate the retributive aspect of God's justice which is involved in his passionate determination to set the world right again. Something within us knows that retribution is necessary. God is not universally overlooking. That said, the greater aim of God's justice is restorative; he does not delight in the punishment of anyone. In this sense, Dexter's retribution is yet an aspect of his deep brokenness. God desires that his creation move past retribution and into restoration.

Dexter's art takes on a particularly sinister quality because he does, in fact, delight in the taking of life. His aesthetic delight in a blood spatter analysis or private viewing of his precious blood slides, while seemingly innocuous, is yet a grotesque expression of his sickness. Dexter Morgan is a broken man with a distorted sense of pleasure. And it is all on wretched display in the kill room when his mouth is open, his breath is heavy, and his release is near. He cuts the cheek of his victim, takes a sample, selects a kill tool. A wire. A saw. A drill. A hammer. A blade.

The butcher's apron and welder's mask are the uniform of an artist at work.

A master in the medium of death.

As our survey of a man called Dexter nears its end, it is critical to hover on this fact, to avoid reducing it or becoming desensitized to it: Dexter is deeply stained. As we hover, it is equally critical to reflect again on our own brokenness through the lens of Dexter's life. We, too, are stained. On our best behavior, we are really just like him. And that's where the gospel begins.

Yet, we have also seen that Dexter is profoundly aware of his own brokenness. As much as he is not able to fully overcome his darkness, he senses its gravity. He knows how desperate his situation really is:

> I've never had much use for the concept of hell, but if hell exists, I'm in it. The same images running through my head over and over. I was there. I saw my mother's death. A buried memory forgotten all these years. It climbed inside me that day, and it's been with me ever since. My Dark Passenger.

Knowing the depths of his own personal hell, he desires to climb out of the pit, to become truly human. He is willing to take leaps of faith in that direction, building relationships with those around him in the hopes that he may feel and become more real. There is light within him, light that was apparent from the very beginning of his story when he would only kill animals and desired nothing more than to please and defend his stepparents. This light breaks through with brighter rays as he learns to love and protect Rita, Astor, Cody, Harrison...and Deb.

In light of these relationships, Dexter is able to uncover and discover his true self. Even the kills take on a more redemptive or restorative tone as Dexter, himself, begins to be restored. In the honest starting place of brokenness, and the committed intent to become better and set the world right again, Dexter and his community form a becoming-truly-human politic for life in the world. And this beautifully illustrates (believe it or not) the essence of what a gospel politic may look like for the Christian community in our time.

In a word, it will look like the opposite of the brazen religious hypocrisy so often portrayed in the media or played out in the Christian culture war. For a parallel here, we need only look to the religious killers in Dexter's storyline. Consider, for instance, Joe Walker, who appears in the first episode of the faith-themed Season Six. Joe was part of Dexter's own graduating high school class, a popular quarterback who got all the girls. A clean-cut guy with Christian faith.

Joe's and Dexter's paths cross again at their 20th high school reunion. Of course, Dexter is not attending the reunion for the throwback MC Hammer tunes and spiked punch. He's there for

Joe. Dexter suspects Joe of killing Janet, Joe's wife and high school sweetheart, three years prior. Dexter and Janet were actually friends in high school - a rare relationship during a tumultuous season of life for damaged, young Dexter. Dexter confirms that Joe is, indeed, the killer by collecting a blood sample at a flag football game after the reunion. He gets the sample with his elbow, by "accidentally" driving it into Joe's nose.

Joe soon finds himself in the dimly lit corridor underneath the school bleachers, plastic wrap binding him to an old scoreboard set up as a table. *The kill room.* Dexter interrogates him about Janet's death, discovering that Joe killed her as a matter of convenience because divorce would be too "expensive." When Dexter uncovers a tattoo of Jesus on Joe's chest, he is incredulous, seething:

> **DEXTER:** *What would Jesus have done? Seriously now! How do you reconcile your belief in a higher power, in God, with what you've done?*

> **JOE:** *What difference does it make?*

> **DEXTER:** *I'm just curious.*

> **JOE:** *So what, I'm supposed to defend my beliefs to you?*

> **DEXTER:** *If you don't mind.*

> **JOE:** *No, I mean, everyone makes mistakes. And, th-they do things they shouldn't do. And, they're only human. But, God, see, God forgives us.*

179

DEXTER: *Really. It's as simple as that? You kill someone, God forgives you for it?*

JOE: *Yes!*

DEXTER: *So I can kill you, and God'll forgive me.*

JOE: *Well, no.*

DEXTER: *But you just said he would!*

JOE: *You have to truly repent!*

DEXTER: *Do you truly repent for killing Janet?*

JOE: *Yes, definitely.*

DEXTER: *Liar.*

Dexter raises the knife over Joe's torso as Joe screams in objection. Dexter pauses. "You don't want to do that," Joe says. "Because if you let me go, God will give you life everlasting." Dexter isn't buying it and trades his blade for a mallet. "You cannot kill me, for God is a mighty fortress! And I have been washed in the blood of the Lamb, and he will protect me!"

Dexter silences him with a single blow to the head, then finishes with a knife in the heart.

Painfully obvious in this encounter is Dexter's inability to suffer religious hypocrisy. Instead, he makes the hypocrite suffer. Yet, notice that Dexter is not operating from the standpoint of self-righteousness. He approaches the kill knowing that he, himself, is a sinner in need of some kind of forgiveness, which is further confirmed in Episode Eight when Dexter receives absolution from the senile Father Galway. That is precisely the point - he is doing something about his sin, subjecting it to a Code, trying to become truly human! Joe Walker merely claims God as his own while he does whatever he pleases, leaning on the certainty of forgiveness and protection as if it is his unalienable right.

Joe's faith is an external mark, ink on the skin; it has no real internal, substantial meaning. It is a "master signifier"[5] that identifies him as a believer while his life contradicts that belief in every way. Joe, then, beautifully illustrates precisely what's wrong with Western Christianity.

Christian community is supposed to be an authentic space in which broken people begin to become truly human in Christ, together. There is the beautiful, robust tension of honesty and aspiration, honesty about our own version of our story and aspiration to live into God's version of our story. There is a collective commitment to movement forward on the unique path to wholeness that Jesus offers. Each time we gather for worship, fellowship, or justice, we are putting off more of our "old selves" and putting on more of our "new selves."

True Christian community is the sworn enemy of religious hypocrisy.

This results in a particular type of political presence in the world. Theologian David E. Fitch sums up this idea in the Introduction to his book, *The End of Evangelicalism?*:

181

"By 'political presence'...I am talking about our corporate disposition in society, i.e., what kinds of people we have become in the world...I develop the thesis that evangelicalism has become an 'empty politic' driven by what we are against instead of what we are for. As a result, we find ourselves often in subtle enjoyments that are perverse. They take the form of 'You see we were right!' or 'I'm glad we're not them.' As a result, our beliefs have somehow shaped us into something incongruent with the very affirmations we gather to proclaim."[6]

A becoming-truly-human politic, because it flows from a becoming-truly-human gospel, results in a different kind of presence. Instead of an "empty politic" that is "inhospitable to God's mission," it is a "politic of fullness" that may "inhabit the world communally with the very disposition of Christ Himself."[7] In other words, it is rooted in the particular type of King that Jesus came to be, the particular means through which he was taking charge of the world, and the sort of Code he was drafting for the community he was forming during his first advent.

An easy way to refer to this politic is the phrase "kingdom of God." Jesus repeatedly made the startling announcement that the kingdom of God had arrived ("on earth as it is in heaven"). But he made the first announcement at his return to Nazareth after his baptism and temptation in the 40-day wilderness. He was 30 years old, about the age one might become a rabbi. He entered the synagogue to do a customary reading during the gathering and spoke these words from the prophet Isaiah:

"The Spirit of the Lord the Eternal One is on Me. Why? Because the Eternal designated Me to be His representative to the poor, to preach good news to them. He sent Me to tell those who are held captive that they can now be set free, and to tell the blind that they can now see. He sent Me to liberate those held down by oppression. In short, the Spirit is upon Me to proclaim that now is the time; this is the jubilee season of the Eternal One's grace" (Luke 4:18-19).

Then, amazingly, "He told them that these words from the Hebrew Scriptures were being fulfilled then and there, in their hearing" (verse 21).

To an oppressed Middle-Eastern people group in the first century, these were nothing less than the words of liberation spoken by the long-anticipated King. Not only Rome's oppression, but the very brokenness of the fallen creation itself - poverty, inequality, sickness, violence, and death - were virtually declared to be over that day in the synagogue. Any first-century Jewish listener would hear the prophetic hope of final restoration in Jesus' reading. He was the King bringing God's restorative justice to the broken world, once and for all.

The particular means through which he would do this, though, was *not* what the people were anticipating. He was the charismatic, dynamic politician declaring himself to be in charge, but he was also a humble carpenter's son, an untrained rabbi. As he would go on teaching and miraculously healing people throughout the region of Judea, he would also urge them to avoid violence (Matthew 26:52). He would warn of his own impending execution (Luke 24:7). He seemed certain that an incredible catastrophe was coming for the capital city of Jerusalem (Matthew 24, Luke 21). These things just didn't seem to square with what people at the time expected from their Liberating King. They wanted a military hero, they wanted to fight Rome alongside him, they wanted him to restore the Temple and rule the world from Jerusalem.

183

God's plan for the Liberating King Jesus was different, even though it was perfectly in line with his plan all along. His plan was for a new exodus and a new Code embodied in a new people. His plan was to work through this new people to bring restorative justice to the world progressively, leading up to the end when all will be restored at Jesus' *second* advent. His plan was for the kingdom of God to be implanted in the world through the Messiah, like a mustard seed or a pinch of leaven in a lump of dough (Matthew 13:31-33). The seed will grow into a mighty tree, eventually. The leaven will produce a wonderful loaf, eventually. But the plan will never, ever pursue selfish power and corrupt control in order to expand and achieve its goal.

Jesus started to enact this plan through his life, death, and resurrection and ensured the final outcome, the full restoration of creation. In the meantime, his newly formed people - the Christian community, the church - were set on a mission to bring more and more health and nourishment to the world. To bring good news to the poor, freedom to the oppressed, sight to the blind, equality to the marginalized. To announce that "this is the jubilee season of the Eternal One's grace."

The new Code to be embodied by this new people was, like Moses' Code, delivered on still another mountain - not Sinai and not Calvary, but an unnamed high place in Galilee where Jesus once spoke to a large crowd. We know it as the Sermon on the Mount. Like Jesus' initial kingdom announcement, this Sermon was revolutionary. It was better than any campaign stump speech before or since, and the legislation introduced there was set to change the world.

"Blessings on the poor in spirit! The kingdom of heaven is yours... Blessings on the people who hunger and thirst for God's justice! You're going to be satisfied. Blessings on the merciful! You'll receive mercy yourselves... Blessings on the peacemakers! You'll be called God's children" (Matthew 5:3-9, KNT).

"You know that Hebrew Scripture sets this standard of justice and punishment: take an eye for an eye and a tooth for a tooth. But I say this, don't fight against the one who is working evil against you. If someone strikes you on the right cheek, you are to turn and offer him your left cheek... You have been taught to love your neighbor and hate your enemy. But I tell you this: love your enemies. Pray for those who torment you and persecute you - in so doing, you become children of your Father in heaven. He, after all, loves each of us—good and evil, kind and cruel. It is easy to love those who love you - even a tax collector can love those who love him. And it is easy to greet your friends - even outsiders do that! But you are called to something higher: 'Be perfect, as your Father in heaven is perfect'" (Matthew 5:38-39 and 43-48).

"But when you do these righteous acts, do not do them in front of spectators. Don't do them where you can be seen, let alone lauded, by others. If you do, you will have no reward from your Father in heaven. When you give to the poor, do not boast about it, announcing your donations with blaring trumpets as the play actors do. Do not brazenly give your charity in the synagogues and on the streets; indeed, do not give at all if you are giving because you want to be praised by your neighbors... Likewise, when you pray, do not be as hypocrites who love to pray loudly at synagogue or on street corners - their concern is to be seen by men" (Matthew 6:1-2 and 5).

185

"If you forgive people when they sin against you, then your Father will forgive you when you sin against Him and when you sin against your neighbor. But if you do not forgive your neighbors' sins, your Father will not forgive your sins" (Matthew 6:14-15).

"No one can serve two masters. If you try, you will wind up loving the first master and hating the second, or vice versa. People try to serve both God and money - but you can't. You must choose one or the other. Here is the bottom line: do not worry about your life" (Matthew 6:24-25).

This is what a becoming-truly-human politic looks like.

This is life in the kingdom of God.

Stanley Hauerwas and William Willimon write:

"Here is an invitation to a way that strikes hard against what the world already knows, what makes sense to everybody. The Sermon, by its announcement and its demands, makes necessary the formation of a colony, not because disciples are those that have a need to be different, but because the Sermon, if believed and lived, makes us different, shows us the world to be alien, an odd place where what makes sense to everybody else is revealed to be opposed to what God is doing among us. Jesus was not crucified for saying or doing what made sense to everyone... Our ethical positions arise out of our theological claims, in our attempt to conform our lives to the stunning vision of reality we see in the life, death, and resurrection of Jesus."[8]

It is a powerful, subversive, surprising vision of reality.

It is strange to write about this kind of kingdom - one in which forgiveness, peace, and enemy-love reign - while simultaneously writing about the serial killer who kills killers. Dexter Morgan has over 100 murders attributed to him in the TV show storyline. He is out for blood, a man of vengeance and retribution.

Yet, we've seen that God, himself, is not universally overlooking when it comes to what is wrong with the world. To say that God doesn't care or doesn't get angry over the world's brokenness is not the point of the Sermon. The point is not to gloss over injustice and evil, but to reveal a goal greater than simple retribution and punishment. The Sermon shows us that in Jesus, the Liberating King, the cold clouds of retribution were driven back by the warm front of the gospel, unveiling the bright sun of grace and forgiveness, ushering in the true and full purpose of God's justice: *restoration*.

Brother Sam is a man of forgiveness.

In the early episodes of Season Six, Dexter becomes friends with Sam, and the ex-convict has a remarkable effect on him. Where Dexter had perhaps become more hardened than ever towards the possibility of God, Sam opens him up to at least consider the transformation possible through a life of faith, especially for the sake of his little boy, Harrison. When Harrison gets sick, Dexter actually prays in desperation - all because of Sam's influence - and Harrison soon recovers.

However, Sam is then senselessly attacked by his own disciple, a Judas-like character named Nick; and he eventually dies from his wounds. But before he dies, Sam and Dexter have an opportunity to speak one last time. The atmosphere in the hospital room is charged:

187

DEXTER: *Sam, I'm here. Don't worry. I know it was Nick who shot you. I'm gonna make sure he pays.*

SAM: *No, don't do that.*

DEXTER: *I don't understand…*

SAM: *I want you to give Nick a message for me.*

DEXTER: *Yes…*

SAM: *Tell him that I forgive him.*

DEXTER: *What?*

SAM: *You're the only one that I trust to tell him. And don't tell anybody. The boys from the shop – they wouldn't…they're not ready.*

DEXTER: *You're wrong – I can't do this.*

SAM: *You can.*

DEXTER: *You don't know me.*

SAM: *Yes I do. I know about your darkness. But I also see your light.*

DEXTER: *If there's light in me, I don't feel it. I just want to hurt Nick. You don't know how much I wanna hurt him.*

SAM: *You need to forgive him.*

DEXTER: *But I don't know how.*

SAM: *Just let it go. Can't live with the hate in your heart – it'll eat you up inside. We gotta find some peace in life.*

DEXTER: *Nick doesn't deserve it.*

SAM: *It ain't about him. Dexter, if you don't let that darkness go, it won't let go of you. Let it go, let it go.*

Some in Dexter's community are closer in relationship to him than others, but regardless, each plays a part in response to his unorthodox leadership. Even the more distant connections are a part of Dexter's politic. Angel Batista's misguided mentoring, James Doakes's belligerent bullying, Vince Masuka's friendly joking, and Maria LaGuerta's secret admiring all join in the interplay of Dexter's agenda to balance the scales, to establish justice, to set the world right again. As one traces the storyline through each of the six seasons, one gets the impression that the whole of Dexter's community is better because of his subversive leadership.

Dexter Morgan matters.

And he matters most to those closest to him. Rita, Astor, Cody, Harrison...and Deb.

189

Deb's passion for justice is different from Dexter's in its origin and motivation. Clearly, Dexter's *execution* of justice follows a different path as well. Even so, they are both broken people on the same path to wholeness. And they are full-blooded partners in a becoming-truly-human politic, passionately determined to set the world right again.

In Season Six, we are introduced to a new element in the plot, apparently on the writers' table for some time now, but only revealed in the final six episodes. Debra Morgan goes to therapy. She goes in order gain a better understanding of why her relationships tend to become so destructive and why she cannot seem to be her true self and live out her passion for police work at the same time. In one conversation with her therapist, Deb begins to break down:

"What do you want me to say? That my life is a train wreck of a disaster?...Well I already know this, this isn't news to me, okay? I already know that I am broken."

The therapist responds, "Do you know that you don't have to be? You can pick up the pieces."

While *Dexter* doesn't deal expressly with the idea of economic inequality, it does deal intensively with the idea of injustice. A becoming-truly-human politic in the real world cannot avoid economic injustice. The church is living smack-dab in the middle of a world in crisis. The question is: does the church matter?

Does the gospel matter?

Under the leadership of the Liberating King, the church ought to be a powerful force for healing the disparity that movements like Occupy are reacting to. And no wonder: recent studies are showing that this inequality is linked to nearly every other social blight, from mental illness to drug abuse to obesity to teenage births to imprisonment rates. Richard Wilkinson and Kate Pickett document this in their book *The Spirit Level*:

"It has been known for some years that poor health and violence are more common in more unequal societies. However, in the course of our research we became aware that almost all problems which are more common at the bottom of the social ladder are more common in more unequal societies. It is not just ill-health and violence, but also...a host of other social problems. Almost all of them contribute to the widespread concern that modern societies are, despite their affluence, social failures."[9]

The United States ranks second in the income gap between the richest 20% and the poorest 20%. The richest 20% bring home *nine* times more income than the poorest.[10] Interestingly, Florida is among the most *unequal* states in the US.[11] (Perhaps this could be used to explain the glut of murderous behavior in *Dexter's* Miami!)

The gospel becomes incredibly relevant when we consider what Jesus was announcing that day in the synagogue. He was announcing good news for the poor through the "jubilee season of the Eternal One's grace." That implied the forgiving of debts, the return of property taken by creditors, the healing of farmland killed by drought. Basically, the end of inequality. This fits the prophetic hope perfectly:

191

"Here's what I want: Let justice thunder down like a waterfall; let righteousness flow like a mighty river that never runs dry" (Amos 5:24).

"Wash yourselves, clean up your lives; remove every speck of evil in what you do before Me. Put an end to all your evil. Learn to do good; commit yourselves to seeking justice. Make right for the world's most vulnerable - the oppressed, the orphaned, the widow. Come on now, let's walk and talk; let's work this out. Your wrongdoings are bloodred, but they can turn as white as snow. Your sins are red like crimson, but they can be made clean again like new wool" (Isaiah 2:16-18).

The becoming-truly-human gospel is embodied in a becoming-truly-human politic in the world. A politic that matters to everyone and everything that is broken. One that really embodies the hospitable, generous presence of Jesus the King. The question, really, is whether the church will look like the one depicted in these passages:

"There was an intense sense of togetherness among all who believed; they shared all their material possessions in trust. They sold any possessions and goods that did not benefit the community and used the money to help everyone in need. They were unified as they worshiped at the temple day after day. In homes, they broke bread and shared meals with glad and generous hearts. The new disciples praised God, and they enjoyed the goodwill of all the people of the city. Day after day the Lord added to their number everyone who was experiencing liberation" (Acts 2:44-47).

"He orchestrated this: the Anointed One, who had never experienced sin, became sin for us so that in Him we might embody the very righteousness of God" (2 Corinthians 5:21).

This becoming-truly-human politic is a humble presence that subversively works for justice in a broken world, bringing healing in spirit, mind, and body. In point of fact, it is meant to be the presence of Jesus himself, continuing the work he began when he first "became flesh and made his dwelling among us" (John 1:14, NIV). And it will entail a uniquely powerful passion for setting the world right again precisely because it is "a politic flowing forth out of an abundance at its core...capable of extending a generosity that comes from beyond itself."[12] It is based in the powerful, overflowing love of the Father, Son, and Spirit. Thus, the poor will be empowered and sustained. The trafficked will be rescued and employed. The sick will be visited and supported. The marginalized will be accepted and embraced. Systems of oppression will be confronted and subverted. New ways of living, consuming, and giving will be innovated. The earth will be cared for and cultivated. And deeply broken hearts and minds will find hope restored in the life-affirming salvation of the Liberating King and his kingdom.

And all of this without the trumpeting of prideful ambition, or the weariness of thankless work. This politic is coming from the Source of justice himself, and it is moving directly into the fully and completely restored world to come. May this restorative justice flow like a river. May a people rescued by the blood of Jesus bring righteousness to a dearly damaged creation.

Theologian Stanley Hauerwas once said, "I'm a pacifist because I'm a violent son of a bitch."[13]

What he means is that he is a broken, violent person, but he has entered a becoming-truly-human community where Jesus is healing his violence. His community is moving forward on the unique path to wholeness, together. And, in turn, the community is expressing a becoming-truly-human politic that brings healing to the world's violence.

Dexter Morgan is a broken, violent man.

Perhaps he would say to us, along with Billy Corgan, "The killer in me is the killer in you."

There is a brilliant invitation in this kind of honesty about our own brokenness.

It's a gospel invitation to become truly human through the blood of the Liberating King, Jesus.

The choice really is ours.

Season Five's main antagonist is a man called Trinity. While his moniker refers to his serial pattern of killing in threes, there is no doubt a spiritual reference here. When Trinity appeared at the start of the first episode, we, the viewers, felt a rush of darkness.

He approaches his victim from behind. She is in her thirties. He is nude. Bringing her into the bathtub, he places her in a choke-hold until she passes out. Then, taking a straightedge razor, he cuts into her inner thigh, severing her femoral artery. He holds her from behind in the tub as she wakes up. She is aware long enough to feel the life leave her.

The blood.

Trinity's kill is a horrific display of selfish power. He indulges his lust for superiority over his smaller, weaker victim, demeaning her to death. In his twisted vanity, he even holds a mirror so that he can see her face as she dies.

The Egyptian and Roman empires play a prominent role in the biblical narrative, providing a striking contrast to the purposes of God in the world. They are paragons of selfish power, gargantuan expressions of the dissocial spiral of destructive independence that began with the representative human beings in the lush, primordial Garden. There are empires like this today. There are smaller empires too.

God has a thing for subverting the empire. There is a King mightier than Pharaoh, but he works outside the usual system of selfish power and control. In God's economy, in his kingdom, in his politic, the executed nonviolent resister is King. The humble are exalted. The meek inherit the earth. The powerful are brought down low.

It is not surprising to learn that Trinity is active in his church. (He even heads up a relief program that builds houses for the homeless, all as a front for his true identity - an empty politic!) Neither is it surprising that he invokes God in the kill room, as we explored in Chapter Four. His fatalistic understanding is that death was coming for him no matter what, and he could not help it, just like he could not help killing. It was all "God's plan."

This is the pathetic rambling of a man who cannot admit that he is obsessed with his own power.

The politic of gospel is the opposite of this. Dexter may not be "all the way" to where he needs to be, but at least he confronts the hypocrite. Subversively, surprisingly, Dexter brings him down.

Because Dexter Morgan matters.

●

Debra Morgan has a foul mouth.

Even in therapy.

But through the morass of obscenity, she discovers truth about her brokenness and a hope for restoration. It is all, really, about relationship. About love. *Her love for Dexter.*

And it is all confirmed when, for the first time, Dexter utters four simple words to his stepsister: "I love you, too."

Even though it is a surprise at first, it shouldn't be. Dexter indicated as much in a narration from the Pilot episode:

**If I could have feelings for anyone,
I'd have them for Deb.**

The Doomsday Killer of Season Six is a religious fanatic named Travis Marshall (played by Collin Hanks). He and his imaginary leader, Professor James Gellar, are convinced that they have been commissioned to usher in the end of the world. They do this by reenacting violent scenes ("tableaus") from the book of Revelation, with each reenactment ending up with someone's murder. It is a brutally self-righteous political campaign against a world of wicked sinners, a numberless, nameless, faceless, enemy "them."

Dexter finally brings him into a rather sacred kill room, set up in the old church that Travis was using as a home base for his twisted politic. While Travis's lust for power is not as pronounced as Trinity's, his hypocrisy is no less offensive. He invokes God, too, in a manner very similar to Trinity, referencing the grand, predestined purpose leading up to this moment while trying to deny its possible outcome. Their conversation becomes an argument that ends with Dexter hinting that perhaps it *was* God's unchangeable plan that put Travis on his table.

Dexter's knife smoothly ascends and descends, plunging deep into the fanatic's chest.

Then, something happens.

Deb walks in.

She sees everything.

Dexter is known, for the first time, by his best friend, the one he loves.

Oh God.

If we are ever going to find our way out of the gospel fog that lays heavy all around us, and if we are ever going to move beyond God's stunt doubles to the real thing, then we must get back to Jesus, the surprising, subversive, Liberating King, and his life- and world-affirming gospel.

If the church is ever going to embody a politic of fullness and not emptiness, and if we are ever going to be free of the hypocritical master-signifiers that often define us, then we must get back to the honest and powerful promise of becoming truly human in the Messiah.

In this way, and in this way only, will we join in God's restorative justice that is breaking into our broken world.

In this way, and in this way only, will we see the world set right again.

In this way, and in this way only, will we see our own brokenness healed and our own emptiness filled.

Because nothing else can make us, and this world, whole again.

Nothing but the blood of Jesus.

Jesus, the Liberating King, summed up his teaching, the true meaning of God's Code, and the politic for his people in two Great Commandments.

Love God.

Love your neighbor.

That's really all there is to it.

Love is at the center of it all.

After saving Harrison's life in the finale episode of Season 6, Dexter whispers to his son, "Whether you're a lion or a lamb, I'll always love you."

We are all broken people.

Broken people with a Father who loves us.

Brother Sam said light can keep darkness at bay.

But I wonder if darkness is defined by light.

If so, darkness can't exist on its own.

There must, by definition, be light somewhere, waiting to be found.

ENDNOTES

FOREWORD

1   Miroslav Volf, Exclusion and Embrace (Nashville: Abingdon Press, 1996), 303, 304.

CHAPTER 1 – A MAN CALLED DEXTER

1   Leah Goldman and Kevin Lincoln, "The New Most Dangerous Cities in America," *Business Insider*, 2011, http://www.businessinsider.com/most-dangerous-cities-2011-9?op=1.

2   All quotes from Dexter are transcribed directly by the author.

3   Augustine, *Confessions*, 1.1.

4   Jerry S. Piven, "Dexter's Mirror," *Dexter and Philosophy*, eds. Richard Greene, George A. Reisch, and Rachel Robison-Greene (Chicago: Carus Publishing Company, 2011), 80.

5   David Kinnaman and Gabe Lyons, *UnChristian* (Grand Rapids: Baker Books, 2007), 182, 184.

6   Scot McKnight, *A Community Called Atonement* (Nashville: Abingdon Press, 2007), 21.

7   Ibid., 23, 24.

8 Gabe Lyons, *The Next Christians* (New York: Random House, 2010), 30.

9 Ibid., 34.

10 Ibid. 50, 51.

11 Sufjan Stevens, "John Wayne Gacy Jr.," *Come on Feel the Illinoise*, Asthmatic Kitty Records, 2005.

CHAPTER 2 – A SON CALLED DEXTER

1 Dwell Missional Church, http://dwellchurch.org.

2 Frank Newport, "State of the States: Importance of Religion," *Gallup*, 2009, http://www.gallup.com/poll/114022/State-States-Importance-Religion.aspx.

3 Wanda Lau, "Holy Hometowns," *Men's Health*, 2010, http://www.menshealth.com/best-life/holy-hometowns.

4 Tim Keller, *The Prodigal God* (New York: Dutton, 2008), xiv, xv.

5 All Bible quotations are from The Voice translation, unless otherwise noted: NIV = *New International Version*. KNT = *Kingdom New Testament*.

6 Tim Keller, *The Prodigal God* (New York: Dutton, 2008), 46.

7 Ibid., 45.

8 David Bazan, "Hard To Be,"
Curse Your Branches, Barsuk Records, 2009.

9 N.T. Wright, *Justification: God's Plan & Paul's Vision*
(Downers Grove: InterVarsity Press, 2009), 128.

10 Tim Keller, *The Prodigal God*
(New York: Dutton, 2008), 44, 45.

11 Chris Seay, audio sermon, Ecclesia Houston, 2009,
http://www.ecclesiahouston.org/messages/podcast-2009-1.

12 Lauren Ober, "Gospel Truth," *Seven Days*,
December 2010, http://7dvt.com/2010dwell-church.

CHAPTER 3 – A FATHER CALLED DEXTER

1 N.T. Wright, *Surprised by Hope*
(New York: HarperCollins, 2008), 196, 197.

2 Chris Seay, *The Gospel According to Jesus*
(Nashville: Thomas Nelson, 2010), 149.

CHAPTER 4 – A HERO CALLED DEXTER

1   Dan Glaister, "Amish school was riddled with bullets
    – coroner," *The Guardian*, October 2006, http://www.
    guardian.co.uk/world/2006/oct/05/usgunviolence.usa.

2   Made Visible, http://madevisible.com.

3   *Nefarious: Merchant of Souls*, Exodus Cry, 2011,
    http://nefariousdocumentary.com/.

4   Katy Waldman, "Character Studies: Dexter Morgan,"
    Slate, January 2012, http://www.slate.com/blogs/
    browbeat/2012/01/19/dexter_morgan_why_do_we_
    really_love_a_murderous_sociopath_.html.

5   Rob Bell, *Love Wins* (New York: HarperOne, 2011), 97, 98.

6   N.T. Wright, *Surprised by Hope*
    (New York: HarperCollins, 2008), 178, 179.

7   Damien McElroy, "Amish killer's widow thanks families of
    victims for forgiveness," *The Telegraph*, October 2006,
    http://www.telegraph.co.uk/news/worldnews/1531570/Amish-
    killers-widow-thanks-families-of-victims-for-forgiveness.html.

8   Daniel Burke, "Amish Search for Healing, Forgiveness
    After 'The Amish 9-11'," *Religion News Service*, October
    2006, http://web.archive.org/web/20061021051654/http://
    www.religionnews.com/ArticleofWeek100506.html.

9 Chris Seay, *The Gospel According to Jesus* (Nashville: Thomas Nelson, 2010), 3.

10 Ibid., 12.

CHAPTER 5 – A BELIEVER CALLED DEXTER

1 Video interview, "The Writer's Room," http://www.sho.com/site/dexter/video.sho?bcli d=594357686001#fbid=XJiyqCxY7Ul.

2 John Howard Yoder, *The Politics of Jesus* (Grand Rapids: William B. Eerdmans, 1994), 215.

3 Ibid., 217.

4 Ibid., 219.

CHAPTER 6 – A COMMUNITY CALLED DEXTER

1 Dwell Missional Church, http://dwellchurch.org.

2 Scot McKnight, *A Community Called Atonement* (Nashville: Abingdon Press, 2007), 121.

3 Rob Bell, *Love Wins* (New York: HarperOne, 2011), 171.

4 N.T. Wright, *After You Believe*
(New York: HarperCollins, 2010), 24, 25.

5 Ibid., 26.

6 Rick McKinley, audio sermon, "I Believe in the
Church," Imago Dei Community, August 2011,
http://www.imagodeicommunity.com/sunday/
sermon-archive/why-i-believe-in-the-church/.

7 Aficionado, "The Things You Like," *Aficionado*,
No Sleep Records, 2011.

8 Typhoon, "Summer Home," *A New Kind of House*,
Tender Loving Empire, 2011.

CHAPTER 7 – A POLITIC CALLED DEXTER

1 Stephen Colbert, http://www.colbertsuperpac.com/.

2 John Howard Yoder, *The Politics of Jesus*
(Grand Rapids: William B. Eerdmans, 1994), 52.

3 NT Wright, *Simply Jesus* (New York: HarperOne, 2011), 10.

4 David Kinnaman and Gabe Lyons, *UnChristian*
(Grand Rapids: Baker Books, 2007), 155.

5 David E. Fitch, *The End of Evangelicalism* (Eugene: Cascade Books, 2011), 26.

6 Ibid., xv, xvi.

7 Ibid., xvi, xvii.

8 Stanley Hauerwas and William Willimon, *Resident Aliens* (Nashville: Abingdon Press, 1989), 74.

9 Richard Wilkinson and Kate Pickett, The Spirit Level (New York: Bloomsbury Press, 2010), 18.

10 Ibid., 15.

11 Ibid., 22.

12 David E. Fitch, *The End of Evangelicalism* (Eugene: Cascade Books, 2011), 126.

13 Colman McCarthy, "'I'm a pacifist because I'm a violent son of a bitch.' A profile of Stanley Hauerwas," *The Progressive*, April 2003, http://findarticles.com/p/articles/ mi_m1295/is_4_67/ai_99818481/.

THE AUTHOR

Zach J. Hoag lives in Burlington, VT with his wife Kalen and two little girls, Gemma and Pippa. In 2008, along with his family and friends, he planted a new church called Dwell (dwellchurch.org) in what is considered the least religious region of the U.S. He serves as lead pastor at Dwell and loves nothing more than preaching through a narrative sermon series Sunday after Sunday. You'll also find him snowboarding at Sugarbush Resort, blogging at zhoag.com, and plotting art and justice initiatives at atmis.org.

213

GRAY MATTER BOOKS

Gray Matter Books exists to promote discussion about matters of faith. Often the subject matter we choose to explore represents gray areas where people of faith might have differing opinions. However, we believe that dialogue on these matters is healthy. Sharing ideas across ideological lines and learning to respect each other betters us as people and believers. Gray Matter deeply values exploration that ranges from the intellectual to the popular culture, and especially how a person's faith is shaped by and continues to shape these areas.

GRAY MATTER BOOKS

www.graymatterbooks.com
8033 Sunset Blvd. #164
Hollywood, CA. 90046
818.934.9998